# Suicide Tsunami

# Suicide Tsunami

*Living in the Aftermath*

SHERALYN ROSE

BALBOA
PRESS
A DIVISION OF HAY HOUSE

Copyright © 2015 Sheralyn Rose.

Photos by Sheralyn Rose
Cover Art by Catherine Garrod copyright (2015)
www.cgarrodart.com

All rights reserved. No part of this book may be used or reproduced by any means, graphic, electronic, or mechanical, including photocopying, recording, taping or by any information storage retrieval system without the written permission of the publisher except in the case of brief quotations embodied in critical articles and reviews.

Balboa Press books may be ordered through booksellers or by contacting:

Balboa Press
A Division of Hay House
1663 Liberty Drive
Bloomington, IN 47403
www.balboapress.com.au
1 (877) 407-4847

Because of the dynamic nature of the Internet, any web addresses or links contained in this book may have changed since publication and may no longer be valid. The views expressed in this work are solely those of the author and do not necessarily reflect the views of the publisher, and the publisher hereby disclaims any responsibility for them.

The author of this book does not dispense medical advice or prescribe the use of any technique as a form of treatment for physical, emotional, or medical problems without the advice of a physician, either directly or indirectly. The intent of the author is only to offer information of a general nature to help you in your quest for emotional and spiritual well-being. In the event you use any of the information in this book for yourself, which is your constitutional right, the author and the publisher assume no responsibility for your actions.

Print information available on the last page.

ISBN: 978-1-4525-2922-6 (sc)
ISBN: 978-1-4525-2923-3 (e)

Balboa Press rev. date: 07/03/2015

# SUICIDE TSUNAMI

"I recommend this book for anyone who is surviving the loss of a loved one. It is a very personal account of Sheralyn's journey through this loss and also other individuals who have experienced a similar loss. They are all very courageous to reveal the depth of their devastation, contributing to a greater understanding and eventually acceptance of the loss. It is compassionate and discusses many aspects of suicide that many people would find difficult to talk about."

Dr Jennifer Rathjen
Clinical Psychologist

"Sheralyn Rose presents a moving and compelling account of the anguish and impact of suicide suffered by loved ones left to cope with such terrible loss. Told with sensitivity, maturity, and compassion, this is a story of love, courage, and life that touches the heart and brings to light the aftermath of, sadly, an increasingly prevalent occurrence. A brilliant book that deserves to be read widely, it makes a landmark contribution to our understanding of the wider implications of suicide and our need to confront mental health issues."

Brigadier (Rtd) Chris Roberts AM, CSC
Author, *The Landing at Anzac*

By the same author (writing as Sheralyn McGuinness)

"Life in a Shoe-Box" in *Taim Bilong Misus Bilong Armi*, (2001), Pandanus Press, Canberra
*Early Menopause. Why Me?*, (2003), Michelle Anderson, Melbourne

# Acknowledgments

Nothing occurs in isolation. The aftermath of suicide is testimony to this. Peter's suicide impacted so many people it is impossible to list them all. Each reached out to do what he or she could to ease the burden of sadness. Rather than omit one person, I would like to offer a greatly inclusive and heartfelt *thank you* to the numerous people who have been connected with this story.

This includes, but is not exclusive to: Liz and Harry Clarsen, Chris and Tim Ford, Wendy Roberts, Jane and Eric Pearson, Gerry McCormack, Mary and Ken Wright, Andy Platt, John Paget, Bron and Chris Rose, Marlena and Michael Jeffrey, Judy and Chris Roberts, Stephanie and Russ Lloyd, Di McGuinness, Cass McGuinness, Jean and Dale Fotheringham, Josephine Blogg, John Blogg, Wendy MacCormick, Julie Najdovski, Mark Cruickshank, Peter Worgan, Kathy Swan, Pam Burton, Joanne Edirnelian, Dianne Clark, Malcolm Cotton, Gaynor Hicks, Jennifer Rathjen, Lucy Brogden, Kath Lavery, Rick Schmidt, the RMC Class of '66, 4 Platoon B Company 7RAR (first tour of South Vietnam 1967–68), and the Brethren of RCDS London 1990.

Some organizations involved were: Wirreanda Nursery, my deepest love and respect for this amazing group of wonderful friends; Northern Beaches Local Area Command NSW Australian Police, with particular thanks to the duty officers who brought humanity into a tough job; NSW State Emergency Services; volunteer firefighters, especially Coal and Candle Rural Fire Brigade;

NSW Scouts; Vietnam Veteran Counseling Service; and Forensic Counselors, Glebe.

To the many people bereaved by suicide who so generously shared their stories, I extend my sincere thanks for their candid honesty and the wish that in the telling, others may gain some comfort.

Thanks also to Cathie Garrod, for allowing me to use her inspiring painting *Tempest* for the book cover.

At the core, however, it is my children, David, Robert, and Larissa, and their families who were, and remain, most intimately involved. Without them, I could never have endured this journey. They make my life worth living, and I know their father loved them beyond measure.

# Introduction

Life can change in an instant. Mine did. It happened one day when a man went to an isolated spot in rugged bush land and took his own life. That man was exceptionally gifted; he was a greatly loved family man, and he had every reason to live. That man was Peter, my husband.

Suicide exploded into my world, a savage, unwelcome intruder, propelling me to a prison of incomprehension and aching despair, shattering my simplistic world where life was for living—not destroying. I grappled with disbelief, repeatedly having to tell myself that his self-inflicted death was real. I tried to find reason where none seemed apparent. I searched desperately for anything that appeared familiar. But everything had changed.

At first, I was numb with shock, unable to absorb the impact of how he had died. Later, a whirlwind of desolation tumbled and orbited around me as the intensity of my heartbreak worked its way into a crescendo. Comfort eluded me, and I was unsure if I could endure the enormity of this catastrophe. Frantically, I tried to maintain some kind of equilibrium, all the while knowing that my life had transformed permanently. Suicide had eclipsed all. I needed answers and searched obsessively for information. Ultimately, this became part of my salvation. It helped dissipate the powerful sea of torment that threatened to engulf me.

At that time, I couldn't imagine feeling happy again, let alone finding meaning in my life. But my slow adjustment and reconciliation is testimony to the incredible healing powers that lie within. Moving beyond Peter's suicide has been mammoth. It has been painful and protracted. Part of me would like to tuck it away somewhere unseen, but knowing there are many others walking in my shoes inspired me to share my story. Living in the aftermath of suicide can be so devastating that many people just close up about it. I hope that telling how it was for me might bring the terrible impact into the open and hopefully, give some solace to those who, like me, felt swamped by doom.

Here I have only skated over the surface, as there are many subtleties and complexities that would make this too long. I wanted to keep my story as simple as possible, as I found that during my period of intense distress, it was exhausting to concentrate on anything too involved. Reaching into the core of my memory, some of it emerges chronologically. Equally much is erratic, as my recollections overlap, entwine, and turn back on themselves. At times it has been almost impossible to tease out specific moments, thoughts, and feelings, as the emotional chaos induced by this violent death sabotaged my ability to reason and think clearly.

It was difficult to talk about openly as well. Suicide is an awkward topic. Once legally and religiously condemned, it has a history of bad press. Prejudice sticks. While there is a degree of intrigue when a public figure suicides, most suicides are not discussed openly, making us feel it is rare. But suicide is common. Throughout the world, someone suicides every 40 seconds. More people succumb to suicide than are killed in wars, violent crime, or on the road. Each suicide leaves behind about nine people who are intimately involved and many others who are affected in a variety of ways. Every day, everywhere someone is lost to suicide. Every day, everywhere, others grieve. Thus my story is not unusual. The silence around suicide does not make it less real. It perpetuates stigma and secrecy; the twin burdens passed on to loved ones left behind.

It was some time before I understood any of this. Although Peter had been anxious and agitated, I hadn't imagined the outcome would be Death. A tragedy. First for him, then for numerous others left struggling in the aftermath. As Peter's life ended, it created a haunting nightmare. I felt I had been swept up by an enormous wave, over which I had no control, no foothold, no means of survival. It seemed everything I knew had been washed away, and I was merely flotsam bobbing about, churning around in a hostile sea, in danger of drowning in the tempestuous waters. I had no concept of the overwhelming dismay I would feel, the absolute chaos my life would become, and the never-ending ache for understanding. All the courage I could muster did not ease my distress.

Emotional wreckage lay everywhere. Unrelenting anguish filled my mind and entered into every aspect of who I was. I became my grief. I absorbed it into every cell of my body. It wakened me at night from fitful sleep, clutching at my chest, weighing me down with its oppressive mass and stealing my breath. That indiscriminate tidal wave had swept away all I held close, leaving a barren and alien shore. I was beginning to understand how suicidal people feel isolated with their extreme suffering. Now I was feeling alone with my heart-wrenching sorrow.

Frightened for my own survival, I forced a superficial calmness as I searched for relief. Reaching into the darkness for pen and paper, I began to write. The written word became my companion as I recorded my feelings in a diary. Then two. Then more. Writing was cathartic. If I put my words on paper, they were outside; I could observe them; they didn't need to devour me.

I was driven to find answers—anything to explain the unexplainable and empathize with the tormented. I needed a framework, a reference point, something to provide an anchor to steady me through the calamity that had instantly redefined my life. I searched the wasteland of self-destruction for a safe haven, somewhere to place my hurt, some way of finding relief from my suffering. I searched for any clue that might make sense of my abruptly altered life.

I read voraciously, everything I could find to help me comprehend the complex array of factors related to suicide. I became aware of how often it appears in literature, art, film, and music, highlighting its universality. Without understanding and acknowledging the existence of suicide, it is almost impossible to accept. I needed explanations, and this became the driving force that took me through a complicated and ever-changing tangle of questions, doubts, loneliness, depression, and helplessness. Disjointed and jostling, these feelings surrounded me, making it difficult to place any of it in recognizable order. I needed to negotiate my own maze of misery until I became acquainted with its convoluted trickery.

Before I could find any sense of resolution, I had to understand suicide as a form of pain relief rather than a rejection of life. On some level, I began to understand the terrible pain that precedes suicide. Suicide is not a vindictive act, but rather it is escape from unendurable agony. Many people look for a single reason, someone or something to blame, like a failed relationship or a financial crisis—events people usually survive. There had to be more. I found that suicide generally comes at the end of protracted and worsening anxiety. Accumulated anguish. Existing deep unrest that finally cannot be tolerated. A particular incident may be the last straw, but rarely is it the only cause.

My obsessive pursuit for answers was beginning to shine a shaft of light onto the darkness of my ignorance. More like a shifting spotlight than a full beam of knowledge. As my gaze followed the illumination, the brilliance I had just seen melted back into shadow. It was a mischievous game. Slowly, a softer light showed a wider picture of what previously had been hidden to me. Perhaps I always knew but didn't want to see. What intuition sensed, reason dismissed.

Gradually, I peeled away layer after layer until I had just an inkling of what had driven Peter to this. What I found were social issues as much as individual difficulties. In Peter's case, his youthful exposure to the brutality of war had a lasting effect. He certainly was not alone with that trauma. Psychological damage from battle is well-documented. Currently, in the United States, military suicides have reached epidemic proportions with reportedly more active-duty soldiers succumbing to suicide than are killed in action. Australia and the United Kingdom also record post-combat suicides that are well above the average in the civilian community. As military suicides remain problematic, governments are perplexed about how to deal with this controversial ongoing human cost of conflict.

Peter had compounding problems. Without doubt his military experiences were extremely traumatic. Added to this he had a strong family history of depression and bipolar disorder. Nature carefully woven through life's experiences. Who can pull apart the threads? Investigating all I could, I came to know him better in death than I had in life. He had tried to keep his anxiety secret while at the same time wanting help. An apparent impasse. Had I known then what I know now, perhaps the outcome would have been different. Perhaps not.

That doubt travels with me. It adds to the blame and shame so readily thrust upon, and sadly accepted by, those personally involved. I wrestled with Peter's method of dying. It gnawed and ate at me. It was difficult not to assume some kind of responsibility, as I believe in the connectedness and strong bonds between people.

Slowly, a matrix unfolded. Not instantly, not incrementally, the deep complexity of humanity took shape and became recognizable. To varying degrees, it belongs to us all. A sensitivity too great to bear alone, which is benign as part of the whole, yet singularly deadly.

These concepts absorbed me and began to provide the platform I was seeking. Without them, I would have to place my untouched sorrow within my burdened soul to fester and rot. I had to find my way out of this seemingly irrepressible grief. I had felt broken beyond repair, however, like a fractured bone, I began to knit. Small threads rejoined me to life. Life came to meet me. Tentative and fragile. Drawing me back to the living took time. It took love. It took determination. But it happened.

I was well acquainted with the emotional paralysis of trauma before I began to understand that I didn't have to remain suspended in fear. Just when I had almost capitulated to the heavy bleakness of gloom, I was awakened by the enticing promise of Life. It took a long time before I gained the wherewithal to accept that my survival depended upon how I interacted with this calamity. Nothing I could do could change what had happened. All I could change was what it meant to me. The will to become more than a survivor, more than a victim of circumstance, drove me toward an eager need for release. I searched for inner peace to help me adapt. This came, and went, in many forms.

Over time, I became aware of acquaintances, work colleagues, and friends of friends who had been touched by suicide. Suicide has few boundaries, and I didn't have to look far to find this sadness. To some degree, a number of these people were already part of my life. We shared our stories. Due to my nomadic life, I talked to people from different countries, including Australia, the USA, the UK, New Zealand, and Japan, reinforcing the international nature of suicide grief. I also attended a support group where others spoke of their experiences. This group confirmed that suicide grief can send people underground with their true feelings.

I was intrigued and asked those who seemed comfortable with the idea if they would allow me to record their stories. It was a familiar process to me. My profession as a medical sociologist drew me to revelations the lived experience could provide. This time it was not an academic study but a mutual involvement that helped disperse some of my own pain and, I hoped, some of the pain of those who bravely opened up to me. Conscious of my responsibility in prompting others to discuss deeply emotional issues, I made a concerted effort not to cause distress. There was always a clear understanding that anyone could withdraw at any stage. Each person has read and agreed to his or her comments being included in this book.

The impetus to collate snippets from these stories commenced. It seemed natural for me to want to represent the impact of suicide through the written word, as I had gained so much insight from reading. My aim was not to detract from the sadness of a life lost but to add to it the distress of those who were connected and for whom life continues. If I could put this on paper, perhaps it could offer some comfort. Thus, evolving from personal experience and a collection of other people's stories, this book began.

Aware that distance from any experience distorts its reality, I tried to maintain the integrity of my changing life and fluctuating emotions by including excerpts from my diary, to illuminate and add meaning to my recollections. Each chapter also begins with one of my own photographs. Even with these inclusions, it is difficult to recapture sick despair, being ambushed by agony, and unceasing angst. Yet the possibility of communicating this in some way that might touch the lives of others, troubled, as I had been, encouraged me.

Although this is an intimate story, it is not intended to be a unique "memoir noir," a dark personal tale. It equally is the story of many, as within today's privileged world a startling number of people struggle with depression, post-traumatic stress, bipolar disorder, and other assaults to their psychological well-being. Some shrug off their demons, others live with a restless mind, and some end the struggle with suicide.

Those left behind can be consumed by grief and the need to understand. Some fall prey to anxiety themselves, as living with, and losing, someone with a troubled psyche can be challenging. Increased knowledge is the only way others can know of the pain, and I felt compelled to represent my excruciating loss as best I could in the hope of reaching others who may be living in the shadow of suicide. Perhaps I could even reach those who may be wrestling with suicidal thoughts themselves, as it has been suggested that understanding the intense heartache created by suicide can dissuade someone from choosing this option. And I hoped to give some understanding to those who come in contact with suicide, either personally or professionally. With more openness, there may be fewer suicides and more support for those who are affected.

This book travels my path. It covers a period of seven years on what, at times, has been a winding, precipitous, and overwhelming journey. The destination moved with the horizon until I realized that the end point is each moment. Not an illusive destination, but now. Each step, difficulty and joy in partnership. Along the way, I have learned to embrace where I am and value what I have, not cling to and form myself around what I have lost, captive to the past.

My tale tells how, painfully, circuitously, I moved from the catastrophe that catapulted me into a new and frightening world to a place where I could live with the unlivable. The voices of others travel with me, and if this book were to continue, there would be new voices, for suicide has not gone away. Sadly, it remains part of the human experience. I hope open dialogue, knowledge, and compassion can go part way toward easing the burden of those abandoned by suicide and dissipate what felt to me like a suicide tsunami.

# Chapter 1

## Missing

There is no true beginning and no absolute end to my story. There is only the middle. Life is lived from moment to moment, until today becomes yesterday and tomorrow, today. The middle became my story when one day was very different from all the others. I don't even know which day it was because the coroner couldn't identify the exact day Peter suicided.

Yet it is that event, that single action, that has made the before "before" and after "after." That day could have merged, as others do, one into the other, instead of colliding, violently, into the next, altering my life as abruptly as it ended Peter's.

At first, I didn't even realize he was dead. On that beautiful autumnal day when he left our home, I had not realized that I would never see him again. We'd been married for thirty-five years, and after decades of moving around the globe, we had settled among caring family and friends. We had a comfortable home, and Peter loved running his own recently purchased business. From the outside looking in, there seemed little to worry about.

Admittedly, his behavior had been a little erratic. He had been stressed, but life has its ups and downs, and I hoped this was just a passing thing that could be resolved by rest or a holiday. I took him away, for what I hoped would be a restorative break, to a mountain resort. He was confused and dejected. Perhaps it was then that he finally decided on his plan.

There were hints, of course, that all was not well, lots of them, but they were hard to grasp—let alone know what to do about them. As life crisscrosses and turns, we see it only in small pixels at any one time. When we are really close, we become myopic, with the bigger picture too vast, too overwhelming to capture in one glance. Later, I came back to these pieces, time and time again, but at the moment I was embroiled in the present.

Peter had been experiencing panic attacks and daily headaches, yet he continued to work twelve-hour days, seven days a week. He had become fretful and pallid, talking obsessively, and inaccurately, about the state of our affairs. He was convinced that our personal financial world was about to implode and, like a house of cards, it would fold around us. By the end of the week, he said, it will collapse. The bank will take everything. Well, he was right in a sense. Our world did collapse, but not as he saw it.

It wasn't until Friday afternoon that it dawned upon me that he was referring to himself. *He* was going to collapse by the end of the week, and here we were mid-Friday afternoon, and no sign of Peter. When he hadn't returned as I expected by mid-morning, I called his mobile. No response. I tried his work; no Peter. Then our daughter. No Dad. I had to give him the benefit of doubt; he could be at the hardware store, or maybe he had stopped in to see a friend, although he hadn't done that for a long time. Then lunchtime came. No Peter. I tried his mobile again. No response.

I saw it then, his mobile, on the kitchen bench, switched off and left neatly beside his briefcase with a bunch of his keys. He had not been seen at his work, and by now several people were becoming anxious. I phoned the local police. No reports of accidents. I was beginning to realize that something was wrong.

Peter was missing.

I called a friend, who called others. Several came to our home, all concerned. Darkness fell. One drove me to the police station. How bizarre it was, standing there, clutching a photo of Peter, reporting that this loving family man, my dearest companion, a man with so much to live for, had disappeared. It felt surreal. Too ludicrous to contemplate. But, of course, being missing is not a crime, and experience has taught the police to be circumspect, so we were advised to wait.

Feeling dazed and discouraged, the unsettled night was one of torturous speculation. Peter could be anywhere, but our daughter was insistent that he was close by. The following morning, she identified several possible locations she thought he might be. Friends and family formed into search groups and set off. As she predicted, his vehicle was found just about a mile from our home, with his little dog inside. He had backed it into the bushes. I presumed that this was to make the number plate visible so his dog could be found. Later, I realized that my assumption was wrong; this was a vantage position where Peter could see anyone approaching. Of course, I didn't understand then that he had reverted to being a soldier in action.

At least now there was a starting point. The police were contacted, and the search began. In the first instance, only specialist teams were allowed into the area. The sniffer dogs, heat-seeking helicopters, rescue police, special emergency services, and volunteer firefighters found nothing. No hint of Peter.

The terrain is rugged with thick, low scrub, and it is difficult to see someone only a few meters away, especially if they don't want to be seen. Late in the afternoon, after the official searchers left, we were allowed onto the site. Walking into the motionless and beautiful moonlit night, I felt ill. I panicked. I wanted to shout, "I can't do this," but I forced it away, knowing I had to do it. I had to try to find Peter, to try to understand what he was feeling.

It was like a dream, a fantasy. I felt strongly apprehensive. *Is this how Peter had felt? Had he thought, "This is it. Now I'm walking away from my life as I know it forever?" Was he frightened?* Of course he was. I could feel it. I could feel his wretchedness, his determination, and his extreme fear.

Then nothing. Silence. Calling his name softly, then louder, then with purpose. "Come home. We love you. Come home." As we stood in the silver moonlight, our voices carried across the valley. He would hear us. He would know we wanted him.

Still nothing.

We followed the trail farther into the bush, and the lantana bushes rose high and leaned over the path, threatening to envelop a loitering passer-by. I could feel him, the soldier, frightened and hiding. He's been here, terrified and quiet. He will not let us find him.

Friends and family worked out search teams, and Peter's little dog joined each relay, exhausted, faithfully ignoring her red, swollen paws.

Nights and days merged.

I began my diary.

***Missing—Day 8*** *ends, and I am beginning to realize that this is happening to me. That a man who seemingly had it all has just walked* away, that his pain was so great he could not feel the love or see the beauty around him.

I try to imagine what he was feeling when he drove away from his home, feigning some sort of resolve to beat the demons in his head. To brush away the unhappiness that had lain still inside, deeper and deeper, till it welled into a consuming beast, an invisible master whose crushing hand was all the more powerful through the illusion of nothingness.

If we only believe what we see, we can sneer at the unknown as if it is malevolent or ludicrous. Don't peek. Don't look inside. Careful what you find. Yourself looking out.

I try and try but cannot know the agony, the resolve, the battle within that alienated him from the security of love, his home and family. I feel the pit in my stomach telling me that this is real.

**Missing—Day 9.** *How can there ever be resolution? How does someone return to daily life when he has so comprehensively and publically rejected it?*

*Exposed! That's how he must feel now. His fear, the blind fear that drove him to seek refuge with the undemanding, the quiet, the spiritual, our eternal connection with nature, has possibly been replaced by an awareness of his disconnection from us. But, what's done cannot be undone, and now he must look for other answers. Maybe he is panicking. Surely he will want to come home now. He will be tired, hungry, and dejected, needing the security of home. How could he have withdrawn himself so dramatically from those he loved? The emerging picture in my mind is his conviction that strong women flourish when they are widowed.*

*Suicide obviously was on his mind. But I do not feel a passing of his soul. I feel his anguish, his fear and confusion. Equally I feel his love, for me and for our children. This must be one of the secrets of his disappearance: his great love. He thought he had failed us. He thought we would be better off without him. How sadly mistaken. If only he could have imagined that to leave us is worse than any difficulty we faced together.*

The likelihood that he had suicided was uppermost in my mind. But there was no body, and without that, I was driven by a well-practiced stoicism not to accept his death without proof. My feelings of unease had prompted me to encourage him to seek professional help. He had done this recently and had been trying to follow the advice given him. Nevertheless, he had disappeared.

Why did I imagine he might return? Why was I "coping"? Why didn't I need sleeping pills? How could I superficially "take it in my stride"? For good reason; I was an army wife accustomed to uncertainty and life on my own. Throughout our marriage, Peter often had been away for extended periods, sometimes in dangerous situations, but he had always come home. Separation was not rare and, most important, I had to have faith in him and keep the "home fires burning" because without that sanctuary, it seemed to me that Peter had no hope of survival. I knew that contact with home, brief and rudimentary as it sometimes was, offered a light at the end of an often treacherous tunnel.

The intrinsic connection of hope, courage, and morale has sustained soldiers throughout history. It is the promise of peace and home that can drive them through horrific experiences and help justify actions that would be anathema in daily civilian life. Families are essential to soldiers, as they are the reward, the compensation for survival. Images of home and loved ones are seared into souls.

This was familiar to me, as Peter and I were both baby boomers and had grown up in the aftermath of war. We were aware that war and separation are unavoidable aspects of military life and were to be tolerated. Like generations before, Peter's turn came with the Vietnam conflict. For me, his absence was protracted agony. Our country's military involvement in Vietnam was not popular, and I rarely spoke of him in my work environment where, for good reason, most supported peaceful withdrawal. The sinking feeling in my stomach started then with the constant anticipation that I would receive a telegram if anything happened to Peter.

I often imagined he was missing in action. Now, thirty-six years later, it was like acting out a nightmare I dreaded over and over and over again. Even though the possibility of death or injury always lurked like a threatening cloud that can suddenly block out the sun, until this was established, it is the lot of army wives to be resilient and ensure that there is a home worth fighting for, an all-embracing and welcoming retreat. Army wives are strong, like their husbands. And so are their children.

Our adult children were already well and truly embroiled in Peter's frenetic and peripatetic lifestyle. Restrained by the family shackles, they loyally orbited around him. Prompted by Peter's fragile emotional state, one son had moved back home, and our daughter nearby. All three children had long ago been drawn into the strange trap of control, discipline, and endurance.

Now everything was disjointed. We were frantically looking for clues to find out where Peter might be and what had pushed him to this. The official police search had finished after three days, but family and friends formed a close group around us. Day and night, they systematically searched different areas of rough bush land. It was unpleasant and dangerous, and we were concerned that one of the search party might become injured. We didn't need further drama.

Days became weeks. The searchers tired and became disheartened. Our children were distraught. Aching. Their lives suspended. We imagined that, if Peter was hiding out, he might risk a fire. Winter was approaching. It was starting to get cold. And wet.

Torrential rain poured for three weeks, the heaviest in forty years. One dark and eerie night, a small group, our children and some friends, returned to one of our favorite spots. The little boys, his grandsons, were asleep in the back of the van. It was like acting out a horror film. Previously dry creeks raged white and tumultuous with a deafening roar that swallowed our calls. Slippery rocks forced us away with their treacherous fortification. What a strange party we were. Clambering around in the deluge, clutching flashlights, and peering into pitch-black, unyielding caves. We had become obsessive.

My children and I were concerned about what would happen if Peter were found alive. How would he be treated? We feared he could be mishandled. It was certainly made clear that he would be categorized as having a mental disorder and placed in hospital. Therefore the children and I devised a plan that, if the opportunity arose, we would conceal him in a place where we would arrange private treatment for him.

Sometimes we felt that he was close by and even watching us. I always left the house unlocked, a light on, and the bed warmed in case he returned, a side entrance open so he could enter without being observed. We left food and blankets out where they could be found easily. We talked of placing signs in various locations or getting a sky writer to send him messages of reassurance. We tried to think of everything possible to help him come home. And at all times, a candle burned in our home to symbolically guide him back.

I had been advised to close our joint bank account, as supposedly, lack of funds can flush out missing people. But I wanted him to have access to it if he was alive. It was, after all, his money, and I wanted him to be able to use it to buy food, a car, a plane ticket, anything he needed. One day, my debit card didn't work. I nearly fainted. I could only think that he had withdrawn all the money, which meant that he was alive! I could barely breathe as I checked the balance and found it untouched. A computer hitch, not an indication of a secret life.

In addition to keeping my diary, I began to see a counselor.

***Missing—Day 15.*** *At last! Help that I need, an understanding of why. Recognition that this is far more complex than a man missing because of business stress or flipped on medication.*

*Talking with the counselor, I can see that all of the characteristics Peter displayed—emotional withdrawal, needing to be by himself, increased anxiety, depression, disrupted family and social relationships—are symptoms of post-traumatic stress disorder.* Peter has displayed these in extreme. Of course, I can see it all so clearly now, but I have been clouded by years of dealing with Peter's anxieties and, quite honestly, fatigued myself from constantly having to adjust everything I ever did to accommodate his need for stability, security, and above all, no conflict.

Armed with this knowledge I walk through the bush again and again, retracing what I presume were his steps, trying to feel what he felt. *Was he consumed by fear and looking for escape? Was he thinking, "the bush is safe, I can hide"?* At night I park where his car had been found and play some of his favorite music, winding down the window, the sound piercing the silent darkness.

No response.

**Missing—Day 20**. *I am starting to mouth the words to myself, "I think he has suicided."* But I find this so difficult to grasp as a reality. The enormity of despair he must have felt to carry out an act that I thought would be alien to him.

"What a waste of life," he had said when a young soldier had killed himself many years ago.

But how would he do it? I can't imagine his fine body violently twisted, now decaying and rotten. The thought has made me physically ill, and I am struggling to continue my daily routine. Of course I do, but it is not only with heavy heart; I also can't find the energy to walk quickly or muster my mind.

*I swing wildly from theory to theory.*

*Was he dead?*

Without doubt he was dead inside. He could never be himself again. Not the strong man I knew. Wherever he was, whatever his fate, our tragic story was well underway.

# Chapter 2

# Discovery

***Discovery—Day 22.*** *My worst fears. It is him, found by children, dead all the while. "Ask not for whom the bell tolls; it tolls for thee."*

*Family, friends, police, all here, comforting, needing comfort. Overwhelming grief, sorrow, physical pain. Disbelief, utter dismay, and inability to comprehend. What was he feeling? What drove him to such loneliness, such violence? How could he be in so much pain? How was his heart so closed to the love and beauty around him? Why so black? So cold? So unreceptive? If only he could have felt it, LIFE, that wonderful gift.*

*We talk and laugh and cry, into the night. The fire drawing us, comforting, bonding us forever. Wine, tears, heartache.*

*The dreadful agony of realization has emerged. The knowledge that this isn't a dream, or someone else's nightmare, has hit. Peter's arduous journey has ended, but ours is in full flight.*

Our home was overflowing with people. It had been since Peter went missing. All helping. All caring. Practicalities needed to be tended to, and in some ways, these were an opportunity to avoid being reminded of the residual dreadfulness of Peter's death. The police had handed the enormous responsibility of telling me that Peter's body had been found to a close friend. What a tough call. It was important that each family member receive support. I was completely unable to do this. I was drowning in my own sorrow.

It was difficult to take ownership of this tragedy. Terrible things happen to other people, not to my husband, not to my family, not to me. Yet our daughter had slept in the bush, night after night, close to where her father's body lay, undetected and rotting. And now one of our sons stayed outside the coroner's morgue to feel whatever it was of Peter that lingered there. Peter's body had been exposed to the elements and, when discovered, his decaying form was taken directly to the coroner's morgue. Visual identification was impossible, so dental records were used. Concerned that viewing his remains would be too traumatic for me and my children, the coroner's counselor offered us emotional support. Evidence of his death, for us, were pungent body fluids seeped into the undergrowth and small fleshless bones that had detached from the body where once they had lived. These awful putrefactions were the only tangible remnants we had of the man who had meant so much to us.

I hadn't quite grasped the significance of Peter's remains being taken to the coroner's morgue as opposed to an ordinary morgue. A coroner investigates deaths that are unusual or suspicious, as it is the coroner who declares if death is due to suicide. Murder sometimes is made to look like suicide and, as those close to murder victims are often the perpetrators, the police need to rule out this possibility. This included investigating me.

One rainy and lonely night, before Peter's body had been found, I sat in a police interview room and supplied a lengthy statement about my most intimate relationship to a complete stranger. How bizarre. My fortunate life turned upside down.

Murder theories were not exclusive to the police. This possibility, with all kinds of scenarios, occurred to several people. Never a theory I subscribed to. To me, these ideas reinforced the disbelief and denial prompted by suicide.

I continued my diary, now after the event.

***After Discovery (AD)—Day 1.*** *The police have his belongings. Do I want them? Contaminated by rotting flesh. Of course, I want all of him. Where is he? Yes, we can take you to where he hid, frightened and alone, determined to commit the final act, severing himself from the here and now, from his mind, from his distorted reality.*

*Fearful and trembling, my son and I are unable to stand. We collapse there in incredulity and horror—the stench, the smell of fear, the agony, the confusion, the loneliness, the bravery, the warrior. I feel faint and sick.*

*I wonder how he felt at that final moment.*

*I imagine him grim, purposeful, and solitary as he shunned his mortal life, acting out his plan of obliteration. No longer would he feel the pain, hear the screams, smell the blood, taste the dirt, or see despair. No longer would his youthful torment, untouched for decades, twist his heart.*

*His determination to be rid of the anguish had set his path, hiding his intention and whereabouts. I could almost feel the calmness slipping, fear pitting his stomach and sweating his palms. I imagined him reaching for the blade, sharp and strong, grasping the handle for confirmation, for reassurance of the reality of his fantasy.* No doubt his dog would have been eager to join in, but Peter was beyond knowing of his connectedness to the living.

What was running through his head? Was he anxious to do it quickly or did he procrastinate? Did he feel there was no chance to turn back? No chance to hear the sweet laughter of children? No chance to feel the tears of compassion? No chance to be dazzled by the sun or taste the salt air? No chance to smell nature's sweet perfumes?

For him, the time had come. Focused and determined. Courage consummate. His instrument of death plunged deep.

His final act complete.

The soldier's heart wept tears of blood.

And so his body died just as his soul had done thirty-six years before. Thirty-six years of numbed aloneness. Thirty-six years to endure his nightmares. Thirty-six years to chastise himself for feeling the fear, for seeing the faces and remembering man's inhumanity to man.

He had tucked it away. The goriness, the horror and feeling of sick despair as the unexpected explosion ripped through flesh and discarded life as a dog sheds water from its coat. He had been in the battle zone just a few days and already had witnessed the destruction of war, the snuffing of life's light as effortlessly as a child puffing out birthday candles. This time, it could have been him. It should have been him. Or so he thought. Survivor guilt.

He recalled that particular incident at parties, where he could not be questioned about the true impact. He would talk to strangers, dispassionately, but not to those who really cared. Too revealing. It reinforced the curse of a complex id, the threat of genetic imperfection, the first anxieties of the boy. His demeanor of steadiness, of dependability and constancy, sheltered a quirky thoughtfulness and unease born of internal conflict. Common human threads woven carefully within his deepest subconscious, frayed edges hidden, retrieval avoided.

*He had tried to mingle but found friendship only with literature, philosophy, and those who mused on the meaning of life. He dallied with altruism, learned the thrill of moral purification through self-discipline and the seduction of introspection. This was the sensitive boy who was thrust onto the battlefield.*

*Traumatized by war, weighed down by depression, a deep emotional wound lay raw and untended until the day he could bear it no longer. It was too late to temper the submerged volcano of inner turbulence that erupted and destroyed his life, creating around him a tidal wave of shock and horror.*

News of Peter's suicide rippled around the globe. Family, friends, and colleagues were dismayed. Flowers, cards, phone calls, and e-mails poured into our home. There were literally hundreds of communications. People told touching and telling anecdotes of how they remembered Peter.

To all of these people, I felt I owed something. I didn't know what. I felt responsible for their pain, their abhorrence at Peter's actions, their having to see the ugliness of suicide. Their support both comforted and concerned me. I tried to keep a record of every thoughtful gesture, thinking that one day, somehow, I could show each person how much their contact had meant to me. I was defeated by the effort of doing this and hoped that those to whom I never responded would intuitively feel my heartfelt thanks. The horror of Peter's loss consumed all my energy.

There was uncertainty over the date of Peter's funeral. The coroner could not release his body until identification and cause of death had been established. This took several days. The high drama of the previous few weeks had longer to run. I was on "automatic" and functioning remotely, inwardly removed from any significant acceptance of what was happening in my life. I mouthed the words, I played the game, I seemed to be in control, but I was terrified of being confronted by it all at once. If I let in too much, it would swamp me. I could only face this dreadfulness a tiny bit at a time.

I longed for someplace I could just be, where others didn't have emotions that were too enormous for me to accommodate. I was overcome by guilt. Not only the guilt often spoken about not saving the person who has suicided but also guilt at the emotional damage others suffered. I gave my best to Peter. I had dedicated myself to him. I was shattered that love was not enough. I could not save him. Now all I could see were the broken people struggling in the aftermath.

Unexpectedly, various people around me began to open up about their own experiences. Little by little, I became aware of others who had lost someone to suicide. I had joined a secret, and surprisingly extensive, club of heartbreak. My curiosity was tentative at first. But like a tongue that can't leave alone an aching tooth, I kept coming back to hear these stories as a way of validating mine. If someone else was distressed by suicide, then perhaps my feelings of confusion, guilt, and rejection were not abnormal.

In some measure, these stories became an emotional barometer as I watched and listened carefully. My longing for commonality, for any inkling of understanding, was insatiable. As I shared the sorrow of others, I changed. A different world opened up to me, where people suffer and survive. I needed to know this. I needed to absorb it into my marrow, to feel the indestructible nature of the human spirit in my innermost being, to accept suicide as part of the human condition. I needed to acknowledge this toxic invader, as fatal as any other unchecked illness.

At last, I felt a connection with others grappling with suicide. I wanted to feel what they felt, to follow their journeys, to embrace their experiences. They helped me understand my own. While individual experiences varied, there was something that drew us together, where the personal became the collective.

Stifled by stigma, shame, and guilt many had not opened up to anyone before. Prejudice had found its mark, ensuring that suicide grief had become a very private affair. I was beginning to realize that the tainted reputation of suicide has a huge impact on grieving.

Thus I came to understand that suicide grief differs from other bereavements. Many of the people I spoke to found suicide hard to accept and had to grapple with their own feelings of accountability. Some felt it was a choice, and this not only allowed blame to fester, it also often left them feeling utterly rejected. I certainly identified with a fluctuating mix of culpability and being discarded, feelings that sometimes I reversed and transferred to Peter.

Although most of us were unaware of our membership, we all had joined a large group, often called survivors of suicide. The acronym for this, SOS, shouts alarm, that all is not well. I wondered if it was the cry for help so often attributed to the suicidal? My own family's needs were raw and disconcerting. Less intimate were the stories of those I knew from a distance, a friend of a friend, a work colleague, or a casual acquaintance. Slowly, over a lengthy period, I accumulated and recorded quite a collection of memories, of heart-wrenching sorrow, of bravery and stoicism. They wove through my own torment, giving weft to my warp. We shared our distress at the finality of a life ended abruptly, deliberately, and often brutally. Overt clues, previous suicide attempts, a history of depression were not enough to prepare for this ending.

Although my awareness of other people's experience began informally, I quickly realized that these stories had richness beyond a personal sharing of stories. There were commonalities and emerging themes. With the permission of each person, I began to record their stories. My academic and professional background had taught me the necessity to address ethical and privacy issues, so I began each recording with an agreement that all written material would be made available to each person and they could remove or change any comment they wished. All the stories here have been read and approved by the person involved. Many have used pseudonyms to protect their privacy.

Dreadful as these stories were, they gave me a sense of belonging, knowing that someone else felt as I did. Leaning forward toward me and almost whispering, Sharon haltingly related her feelings at finding her husband dead:

*My stomach was churning as I got out of the car. I didn't know why, but I felt something was different. I saw him straight away—in the doorway. His face was distorted, and he was just hanging there—not moving. I think I just stared for a while—it was probably only a couple of seconds, but it felt like a lifetime. Well, it was a lifetime. It was ours, and it had gone. I was completely matter-of-fact. Just walked past him into the kitchen, dialed emergency, and got a knife. I dragged a chair over and tried to cut him down. I don't know why because I knew he was dead. But I didn't want him there—in our doorway. Why there? But it was too hard, and I stopped and collapsed on the floor. I was still sitting there when the police arrived. That was over three years ago, and I feel worse than I did that day. I felt the pain later, and now I'm never free of it.*

Sharon

The horror of discovery cannot be underestimated. *Why would someone we love, and who we know loves us, do something so cruel? Not only to themselves but also to us?* Traumatic as it is to find the body, or for someone else to discover the body, some suicide victims are never found. Kids who just walk away, mothers who vanish, fathers who disappear and leave no trace; each leaving behind a legacy of torment for their families and friends. There are many reasons people go missing, and for each who does someone lives in hope that they will be found, alive or dead, but found, so that some form of resolution is possible.

A missing person creates all sorts of complications. I needed to find out my legal situation when Peter vanished. I was amazed that where I live, someone has to be missing for seven years before they can be declared dead. Living in limbo.

Others had to deal with the misery of protracted disappearance. Petra's story of her family's unending search for her teenage daughter was heart-wrenching:

*It has torn our family apart. We never found her body, but I still live with the expectation that she will just walk back in the door the same way she just walked out. When her clothes were found neatly folded by the water, we thought she had gone swimming and got into trouble. Then we thought it was some sort of hoax, and she had wanted to leave home and was trying to fool us into thinking she was dead. But we have tried to track her down in every possible way, even overseas, but no sign of her.*

*It took me over two years before I even let the idea of suicide settle in my mind. But I have talked to many people, and even though some suggested it in the beginning, I rejected it outright. I mean, what possible reason would she have to do such a thing? Slowly I began to accept that she had appeared to have signs they say suicidal people have. Like she was a perfectionist—drove herself to achieve the highest marks and was never happy with second-best. And of course it was just before her finals, and maybe she couldn't take the pressure of not doing as well as she expected. But she didn't even do her last exams, let alone wait for the results.*

*I still get confused by it. But we did, well my son and I, go down to the spot, a few months ago now, and we placed a bouquet of flowers in the water. It sort of helped. I watched them bobbing and floating in and out with the waves and came to face, just a tiny bit, that she was gone. But it hasn't made that much difference really. I have left her room, even though our house is small and we could use the space. I couldn't bear it if she came home and it looked like she didn't live here anymore. The counselor told me she most likely has committed suicide, but in my heart of hearts, I can't accept it.*

Petra

Not knowing seemed cruelest of all.

Like Peter, other people had not been found straight away, leaving their families existing simultaneously in hope and terror.

*The whole thing was horrendous, breaking into the flat and finding her sprawled on the bed. The smell was terrible. She must have been there for days. It was unbelievable.*

Joanne

Death does not always occur immediately and James's story of his sister showed me that some people could be maimed or severely injured.

*Her neck was broken in the fall, and her legs and pelvis. She never regained consciousness, and eventually life-support was withdrawn. We were all there when it happened. I don't know what is easier quite honestly. Some feel it gave us time to get used to the idea that she had committed suicide. I found the entire thing disturbing, a memory I carry with me all the time.*

James

I was beginning to get a sense of the vast array of experiences. As my nightmare unfolded, I clutched at these stories. I wanted to see the faces of the disenfranchised, to feel their pain, to remind myself that I belonged to this company of walking wounded and, hopefully, somewhere, to see the possibility of recovery. I continued with my obsessive quest to find an answer.

# Chapter 3

## Questions

Peter had reached out. He was anxious. He was depressed. And of course we had learned posthumously that he had post-traumatic stress disorder (PTSD). As a family, we were all entangled in his frantic restlessness and were as confused as he was about what to do about it. Death by suicide requires commitment. It requires secrecy. To take the journey voluntarily and alone is a desperate departure. No loving farewells to ease the transition, just a furtive and absolute alienation from the living.

I knew so little about the terrible torment that had consumed Peter's life. I needed to come close, to try to understand. Popular images of suicide did not reflect what I was now discovering. I learned that, although some suicides appear to be the result of impulse, many follow a protracted period of emotional anguish. This was terrible knowledge. Of course there was agony at the end, there had to be, but how long had this suffering been tolerated, hidden and capricious?

***AD—Week 6.*** *The memories I had tucked away creep in, like a rolling fog, the damp chill working its vaporous way in through the pores of my skin. Glacial. His sorrowful eyes, his drooping shoulders, his tentative touch. Not a word was spoken, but it was a plea. I was aware only of what I could absorb. More desperate than I knew. I comforted, I soothed. Or so I thought. The swirling, intangible pain had lived in every organ, every tiny space, every cell: invisible, formless and deadly.*

I heard the expression "psychache," the emotional pain that can precede suicide, for the first time when I was interviewed by a researcher soon after Peter's death. It explained a lot. This misery of the mind can vacillate and vanish. Or it can linger, recurring spasmodically, and become unendurable. It can escalate to crisis level, where relief only seems possible by removing its source: oneself. Not only emotional, psychological, or psychic pain, it also can be physical. Headaches, chest pain, palpitations, panic attacks, and confused thinking may accompany emotionally debilitating symptoms. The researcher told me how some suicidal people describe the feeling of sitting in a cave where they observe life but are unable to participate. We literally had searched for Peter in numerous caves. The analogy did not escape me.

While I could understand psychache on a logical level, it still seemed inconceivable that Peter had departed abruptly, without ceremony, and apparently willingly. I had not wanted to accept the possibility of his death. I saw only what I wanted to see, what I was able to see, and what I felt I should see. Even his history of emotional turmoil, having been treated for severe clinical depression, and his eventual disappearance had not prepared me for his final choice.

*How could Peter have done this?* How could others—dearly loved sons, daughters, fathers, mothers, brothers, sisters, husbands, wives, partners, family members, friends, or colleagues—have sacrificed their lives? It was still some time before I could take this in as a form of escape from incrementally worsening emotional and sometimes physical torment.

Although the days, weeks, and months prior to Peter's death were intense, I began to accept that his problems had been even more longstanding than this. Hindsight provided the clarity that had escaped me as I lived alongside his anxieties, when the children and I had been entangled in his misery. I found it difficult to understand how life could seem so bad that the only solution available was death. I wanted to know why Peter could not find effective help. And I wanted to know if I could have prevented his act of self-destruction.

Until I could reconcile these questions, I could not begin to adjust to my new life. My thirst for information was insatiable, yet even as each puzzle piece fell into its allocated spot, I found it difficult to merge these with the image of the person I thought I knew so well.

As I rearranged the pieces, a new picture was forming, one that didn't quite match the image I had of Peter. The Peter I was seeing now was troubled, intent on not sharing the depth of his suffering. Where I had seen strength lay fragility. Where I had seen inclusion lay secrecy. How I ached for the familiar fairy tale where such concealment did not exist. The past had now been snatched as ruthlessly as the future.

I read about the seemingly endless categories of people who are prone to suicide: those with PTSD, bipolar disorder, depression, and reduced levels of serotonin, as well as people from certain age groups, cultures, and political beliefs. Trauma experienced by professionals, such as the police, health workers, and the military, can devastate them to the point of absolute despair. Even pregnant women are more vulnerable to suicide, and murder, than they are of dying from pregnancy-related medical conditions. And as a dispossessed and isolated group, Australian Aboriginals are succumbing to suicide, previously unrecorded in their culture.

Statistics show that not only are men more likely to complete suicide than women, they also choose more violent methods. Some people are motivated by unwillingness to live through a terminal illness or difficult life circumstances. Others may be persuaded by peer pressure.

Supposedly, many people occasionally think of suicide, and a significant number of people actually do attempt this. Fleeting thoughts of "ending it all" can indicate emotional unrest that could result in suicide. Or it might not. How does anyone know when someone's desire to suicide will become a reality? Usually they don't, and very likely, neither do many of those who attempt suicide. Judging from suicide letters, the actions of people who complete suicide, and the comments of those who don't, there often is ambivalence toward suicide. The commitment to proceed can vacillate and waver. It may be a back-up plan, in case internal pain becomes too much to bear, but it might never be acted out. Or it may.

Many people believe that there are other options. Suicide prevention programs are based on evidence that, given time and appropriate treatment, the strong desire to suicide can diminish. Suicide has even been described as a permanent solution to a temporary problem. This is cold comfort for those of us who have lost someone to suicide, as it reduces a complex situation to a simplistic cliché. Of course the impetus may return, and often it does, as is evidenced by those who make more than one attempt on their lives.

These are called "failed" suicide attempts, as if the action that finally leads to self-death is a "success." When a person who is an integral part of our lives is "successful," it can be devastating.

Being bereaved by suicide also increases the risk of suicide. A number of people I spoke with mentioned that they had thought of suicide themselves. Tammy told me she doesn't talk about her partner's death much, as most people find it distressing and don't know what to say. He had gassed himself in his car, and clearly Tammy was deeply affected.

Close to tears, Tammy described her struggle with suicidal thoughts:

*I can't believe I even thought of doing it myself. That is not who I am. But I was so overwhelmed by grief and the horror of finding him. I thought life was just so awful. I really did think about it. I can't really say why I didn't go ahead. Maybe it's because I have a strong faith. I don't know really.*

Tammy

I found trying to reduce suicide to a single cause unsatisfying. Many times, I've heard people say that someone suicided because a girlfriend left them or they were in financial difficulties—or blame it on other stories of woe. I was even led to consider this myself about Peter. Situations like these may appear unresolvable when you are in the pit of despair, and this can trigger a final decision. Usually this happens following protracted and worsening anxiety. Accumulated anguish. Deep unrest that finally cannot be tolerated.

I wanted to look beyond the obvious and ask why someone's girlfriend left or why they were in financial difficulties in the first place. I read that depression and confused thinking prior to suicide can adversely affect relationships and decision-making ability. After all, broken relationships and financial difficulties are not unusual. They may be devastating, but they are not life-threatening in themselves.

Blaming someone for the death of a person he or she loved is unfair and hash. But these accusations came up time and time again in the stories I was hearing.

Tracey told me of the lack of understanding that led to a relationship breakdown with her boyfriend's family.

*His sister wouldn't stop asking me why I had let him do it. As if I could have stopped him, or even knew what he was thinking. It was a double hurt. I realize now she was hurt and confused herself, but I have never forgotten her lack of compassion for me.*

Tracey

What was emerging for me was an increasing awareness of the tenuous interplay between people and survival. I was beginning to appreciate the immense challenges Peter had faced. Nevertheless, it is not necessarily *what* happens to someone but *how they react* that is critical. Rather than the actual circumstance pushing someone to suicide, they are more likely to have been unable to endure the emotional pain caused by it.

It seems that when people experience internal turmoil, they may attempt to gain stability by trying to keep order in things around them, like other people, their work, their home, or their bodies. If external things, such as a relationship or financial loss, cannot be controlled, this could prompt feelings of powerlessness. These feelings can become overwhelming and exhausting. Seeking relief though suicide may appear a viable solution to seemingly intractable problems. It might be tossed around as an option for some time.

During this period of vacillation, it appears that many people seek help, often in a tentative or oblique way. They may make comments that are called "invitations," as subtle hints that all is not well. At the same time, they may wish to keep the possibility of suicide a secret.

Peter certainly gave many indirect "invitations" to a number of people. What a dilemma trying to communicate these terrible feelings while simultaneously trying not to be too overt, in case the ultimate means of control is removed. *Wanting help but unable to ask openly.* As an unwitting conspirator, I had not wished to see how extreme Peter's agony had become. Yet my daughter had warned me time and time again and my son had locked away Peter's firearms. As a family, we were treading a fine line between recognizing the complex anxieties that can end in suicide and not knowing what to do about them.

Peter had always been exceptionally strong-minded, and I found it difficult to challenge the status quo. How do you propose to someone like Peter that you think he has a serious psychological problem? I was worried about undermining his confidence. I was also mindful that physical illness can cause changes in behavior and didn't want to make the assumption that psychological issues could be the sole problem.

"Do you really think I need help?" he had pleaded when I suggested that he, or we both, seek professional advice.

Reluctantly he agreed and was diagnosed as having severe clinical depression. Peter was a proud and successful man, unused to what he would have thought of as failure. Therefore it must have been confronting for him to acknowledge that his troubles lay within. Revealing any difficulty takes courage, yet he consented to the standard treatments of counseling and medication. These therapies are not instant fix-its; they need time and commitment to work. Peter had commenced both of these a few days before his death. Divided opinions arose afterward, as some thought the antidepressant drugs had pushed him to suicide. Others believed that he was already suicidal when he started the treatment and sank further into the spiral of gloom. Perhaps the treatment was too late for Peter. I will never know. Needing treatment could also have compounded his feelings of defeat and disease.

Ultimately, he found his own answer. I believe that shame and feeling he was protecting us encouraged him to keep the severity of his struggle to himself. He clearly experienced tension between maintaining his secret while at the same time hoping to recover.

With the extent of his internal conflict remaining unrecognized, I had little idea how critical his needs were. Although I am now aware of "direct and indirect invitations for help," knowing how to respond can be perplexing. Yet with timely and appropriate treatment, people with depression and suicidal thoughts can be helped. Subsequently they can lead contented lives without being tormented by destructive demons.

The generic term "depression" covers a wide range of conditions. There are different types of depression, and not everyone who is depressed is at risk of suicide. Once hidden and considered a personal fault, depression is now better understood, openly discussed, and has shed its shameful status. However, even with readily available treatments, depression remains a major cause of suicide.

PTSD can prompt suicide as well. The pain of a wounded psyche often is the hidden aftermath of anguish that might never leave the deepest realms of many who are involved in life-altering trauma. Experiencing trauma where your life, or the life of another person, is threatened or is at risk of serious injury can cause responses of fear, helplessness, and horror. These feeling can become embedded, emerging haphazardly at a later date.

Understanding some of the causes behind suicide was helping me. I could see that even though suicidal people may reach out for help, it is not always overt, and people who complete suicide go to great lengths to conceal their intentions. If they did not, someone would attempt to stop them. So, often, we are left only with disjointed clues that are not always easy to decipher. Sometimes, as with Tim and Mary's son, the clues can be hidden almost entirely. They spoke openly of their heartache, confusion, and guilt:

*It is still impossible to believe. Our son had everything. He really did. He was our only child and would have inherited everything we have. But more than that, he had a good education, was popular, good looking, and starting at a very good law firm. He had done really well at university and had no trouble getting a good position. Not so lucky* with the girls though. He had a pretty young thing a few years ago, but it didn't amount to much. He was focused on achieving.

Well, he blew his brains out. Right there on the front lawn. We had just had lunch. He didn't seem much different to usual. Maybe quieter. But he just calmly got up from the table, got his damn gun from the garage, put it in his mouth and bam, killed himself outright. And there we all were, sitting around the table still, when we heard that God-awful sound. I rushed through the front door, Mary was at the window, and my aunt and Mary's dad were dazed and not sure what was going on. I could hear Mary's scream through the glass.

I am tortured by why he did it. Was it our fault? Did we expect too much? I read his diary. You don't expect a boy to keep a diary, but he did. It was full of melancholy, but he had seemed quite content to us. I suppose he suffered from depression. Well I think that because I've read a great deal about it now, and from reading his diaries it makes you realize he wasn't that happy after all. He must have been a master of disguise to keep it from us so successfully. There's no logic to it. I guess he was just excessively sad.

Tim

Without being mind-readers or physically restraining someone, it may be impossible to prevent a person from suiciding. As a family, we lived helplessly with Peter's deteriorating condition. On one level, I knew that something terrible was overcoming him, and on another, I tried desperately to retain some semblance of our usual life, hoping he would magically get better. By this stage, we were in crisis control, and I had taken to not letting him out of my sight. He fooled me completely when he disappeared. This was heartbreaking and created my own feelings of guilt and failure.

However, the decision to suicide was not mine. I came to understand that many people who suicide are not seeking death; rather they are seeking relief from persistent psychological or physical pain. The best I could do now was try to understand and accept Peter's death as the result of terrible and protracted emotional turmoil. I came to acknowledge that the process that leads someone to suicide most likely also makes it difficult for him or her to appreciate the consequences of that action. Sometimes the impact of death can be projected, but usually there is little concept of the depth of despair felt by those left behind. Some suicidal people even feel that their death may be helpful and remove a burden from those close to them. I believe that Peter had thought this. It couldn't be farther from how I was now feeling.

# Chapter 4

# Answers

Peter often sang poignant and sad songs, some referring to removing emotional pain. I knew he was troubled. Was he telling me of his solution? I thought about it afterward. Was this another clue? If so, it had been slipped quietly in while he hid behind a sultry pensiveness. I needed to know more. Understanding came to me in dribs and drabs. I was dedicated to my mission of explanation. I read insatiably, I spoke to many people. Snippets came from all over. I had failed to comprehend the true impact of Peter's life experiences, and now they were coming together like a fragmented jigsaw puzzle. At times, I felt like the pieces had been waterlogged, swollen, and scattered, so that even when they were collected and placed together, they didn't always align smoothly. Sometimes it felt like a 3D image, where you need to stare until your gaze goes out of focus before you see the hidden picture. And of course, through it all, Peter's voice was sadly missing.

By now, I was well aware that Peter's story is not new; nor is it one that will go away. It is the story of our eternal struggle with life. Teasing out the knotted twine that bound Peter, I could see that each strand in its own way strangled him just a bit. Singularly, not enough to pull him down, but as each wound over the other, he became lost somewhere in the midst of its oppressive mass. Rather than peeling off each layer, gently, slowly, he burst forth, releasing his brewing turbulence like a volcano spewing its lethal innards. Peter became victim to his own sensitivities and the invisible ramifications of war.

Psychological damage has long been recognized as a consequence of military action. Given the negativity and stigma placed upon mental disorders of any kind, a derogatory attitude to psychological problems is common. This negativity not only influences military attitudes, it also discourages individuals from admitting that they may have difficulties. Soldiers must not only be tough physically, they also are expected to be superhuman emotionally. After all, war is merciless, and vulnerability will be exploited. Such is the nature of man.

Like many young men in the '60s and '70s, Peter had "served his country" in the aggressive conflict that occurred in the Republic of Vietnam. History changes in the telling. For many years, Vietnam lost its status as a country and was spoken of as a "War." Politically speaking, though, the bloody conflict was never declared a war. This classification worked against our young soldiers. Confusion arose when they returned home to public disdain, ensuring that the horrors these young men had experienced, many forcibly conscripted by the government of the time, remained concealed in the trash bin of their psyche.

Peter certainly kept his wretchedness well hidden. Before his departure, he had expressed his dilemma at following his profession while abhorring violence. Within a few days, he had several firsthand experiences of horrific and gruesome killings. Safe and uncontaminated, home was a long way off.

Throughout his life, Peter felt that his greatest achievement was bringing his platoon back from Vietnam alive. It appears that they thought so too. One of them had everyone at Peter's funeral spellbound with his story of their combat experiences in Vietnam. He opened a chink in what has largely been an impenetrable wall of silence and allowed a glimpse at tucked-away memories and tightly-held emotions:

*Peter was on the advance party for [his battalion], and he and another soldier joined us at the construction of the infamous minefield to get a feel of the country. On Peter's first night in the field, he shared a spot with me in our platoon harbor position, and not long after stand-down, a couple of enemy probed our position. After a brief firefight, we killed them. I remember Peter saying to me that night, "I've been to war, had a firefight; they can give me my medals now and send me home."*

*The following morning, one of the men from my section stood on a jumping-jack mine and was killed instantly. Two others were badly wounded. As Peter was pretty close to the dead, we both, plus one of the others, probed our way to the wounded to dress their wounds and reassure them and remove them from the minefield. Later, we removed the body and wrapped it in a hootchie [a waterproof camouflage material that can be used as shelter] to have it evacuated out.*

*Peter had tears in his eyes.*

*The next morning, Peter was standing a few meters from a young officer who stood on a jumping-jack mine, which killed him. Peter's life* was spared due to the other officer taking the full blast. Two of us started to probe our way to the body, trying desperately not to set off another mine and blow ourselves to pieces. Peter yelled out, "Stay where you are. I will get him." Peter probed his way to [the dead officer] and stayed with him until his body was removed.

[Another time] ... a very fierce battle began with all types of incoming fire ... [After the battle] ... I just knew that Peter would delegate our section to bury the dead enemy. The ground was like rock, so needless to say, the graves were not very deep. Before we moved out from our position, we observed Peter go to the graves. He had put two sticks together by tying them with a hootchie cord to resemble a cross.

He put them on the graves, said a few words, and gave a quick salute.

At the time, it meant nothing to me, but with the passing of time, I reflect back on how honorable this young Australian officer was, the respect and solemnity he displayed for another soldier or officer, albeit the enemy, who had been trying to kill us a few minutes before. Peter always made us bury the dead enemy.

On another occasion ... Peter volunteered [three of us] ... to check for river crossings that a so-called ten thousand enemy were going to cross. I remember protesting to him, telling him he must have overdosed on anti-malaria pills. Fancy sending three blokes out to find ten thousand enemy.

I have never been so scared in my life. ... Fortunately, ... we got back safely, and when we reported to Peter, he put his arms around us, such was the tension he had been through, committing us to the task and the sense of relief that everything had gone okay. Such was Peter's love for his soldiers.

Peter was a great soldier, a brilliant leader of men ... he loved his soldiers, and his soldiers loved him. ... We would have followed him anywhere, and we did, such was our love and respect for the man.

Many people here today will question why Peter chose the path he did, taking his own life; I don't, and nor will any of his Vietnam veteran *brothers, as so many before have chosen the same path as Peter, taking their own lives.*

*The records will not show it, but Peter is but another casualty of the Vietnam War.*

*I say to my fellow Vietnam veteran brothers here today: Please don't be the next casualty. Pick up the phone and call one of your brothers and talk about it.*

*Peter, thank you for taking us to war, and a special big thank you for bringing us home safely. You are our hero.*

Ken

On his close encounter with man's inhumanity to man Peter poured out his feelings of shock, helplessness, and fear to a colleague. Then silence. Unseen. Unspoken. His mission continued. His misery compounded. His voicelessness was confirmed. He told me later that what I didn't know couldn't hurt me.

Clearly, it had hurt him.

Peter was twenty-two years old, and PTSD had begun its dreadful, sneaky invasion. PTSD didn't have that name then, and other classifications of the psychological reaction to battle, like shell shock, combat stress, and soldier's heart, were dismissed as weaknesses. Decades later, Peter described his feelings as having an "aching heart." But a young professional Army officer from an elite establishment was hardly going to succumb to the so-called indulgence of freaking out at the sight of blood. Besides, there was no time for pampering oneself in something as nebulous as feelings; everyone needed to be constantly alert in the kill-or-be-killed situation.

On their return, those of us living with veterans had no idea they could be so terribly and permanently damaged. Even if we did, we were unaware of what telltale signs to look for or what we could do about it. Of course, there are recognizable signs and symptoms that give a sufferer away to the professionals, but individual soldiers and their families are not always aware of the significance of the subtle hints of a mind in turmoil. So implanted are the wounds, and so intent is the individual on avoiding his or her demons, that any hint of disturbance can remain submerged for years.

It was Peter who first suggested, in a throwaway manner, the idea that he had a pre-existing vulnerability to post-traumatic stress. Not intended as a topic for discussion, it was one of the puzzle pieces I dragged from my memory after his demise. He was right. Layer upon layer. What an onslaught he had suffered. Underpinning Peter's distressing war experiences was his own background.

I read that some people are more prone to have stronger emotional responses to life events than others. This seemed to make sense to me. Apparently, even before a baby is born, the way that person will respond emotionally later in life is already being developed. While this continues to develop throughout life, it is most significant and accelerated during early childhood. This sort of information affirmed my own understanding that we are all subject to an intricate interplay between chemistry and culture, the exquisite fusion between nature and nurture. This conundrum leaves even the experts baffled. Nevertheless, some stressors and perhaps psychological problems can predispose certain people to PTSD.

Peter had thought about this. His diagnosis of severe clinical depression, while consistent with PTSD, is not a cause of it. Nonetheless, Peter was convinced he had a mental illness of some kind, and, after filling out a questionnaire on depression, he solemnly told me that he had a score of ten out of ten. As if this weren't enough, I learned how certain illnesses can damage the brain and make some individuals susceptible to depression. From as long ago as 500 BC, clinical reports describe long-term mental impairment following malaria. During the expansive days of the British Empire, medical studies of troops stationed in India identified malaria as a leading cause of mental illness. More recently, studies of Vietnam veterans show that those who suffered cerebral malaria have a greater incidence of PTSD than those who were wounded physically in combat.

Cerebral malaria causes inflammation of the brain and can leave it partly damaged. Long-term neurological problems can occur, such as depression, impaired memory loss, personality change, and a heightened propensity for violence. Many Vietnam veterans have reported these symptoms, which often are treated strictly as PTSD. Many soldiers from the USA suffered from cerebral malaria during the Vietnam conflict. Australian soldiers contracted cerebral malaria as well. One of these was Peter. Toward the end of his tour, Peter became delirious with fever and was evacuated to an American field hospital. His temperature raged for days, and he was packed in ice with a fan to aid the cooling process. He was not expected to live.

He described the days he spent in hospital as frightening and surreal. He did not expect to survive the ravages of this disease either. Although he did survive, he maintained consistently over the next three and a half decades that he was never able to think in the same way as he had before contracting cerebral malaria. He had recurring delirium tremors for years afterward.

Once, after Peter's death, when I was watching a TV documentary, I saw footage of a medical evacuation where I thought I recognized him. The circumstances fitted what he had described. How sad. How poignant.

***AD—Month 2.*** *My heart sank. Stunned. Stirrings of a memory caused my heart to race as Peter's words had painted the picture before me. Exactly as he had described: helicopters, stretchers, tent hospital. Then panning in on a wan, pinched face. So like Peter. Could it be? Coincidence or not, it had happened to him, so might as well be, symbolically at least.*

*I ached for his pain, for the pain of other soldiers. Alone at home, I had never comprehended. How could I? Spasmodic letters, reel-to-reel tapes, one three-minute phone call in thirteen months. Separated by more than distance: We were separated by experience. No e-mail, texts, digital photography, or cyber-communication like Facebook, FaceTime or Skype. Peter existed in my head and heart, in the loneliness of my imagination. I knew only that it hurt; that I was just twenty and alone.*

*I lived for those scant, short letters, covered in red dust and smelling of tropical moisture.*

*Lonely nights with one small, static, mute photograph. I knew that the man I loved lived in a rubber plantation in the middle of a jungle. I didn't know he had already tasted death, horror, destruction—the baseness of humankind. And I didn't know that his entire being, his wholeness, had been well and truly compromised.*

Revealing as all these puzzle pieces were, it was equally amazing that Peter had not only survived but also had a successful and seemingly satisfying life afterward. Along the way, there were now-obvious signs of his distress, such as sleeplessness, super-alertness, and nightmares on return from Vietnam that stayed with him throughout the rest of his life. What conflict he must have felt as the capriciousness of life tumbled around him and he strove vainly to bring it to order. His intense need for control belied the gentle man who dwelt within. I recall how he felt about remembrance days. "Every day is Anzac Day," he would say quietly. There were tears at burying the family dog in the garden. "This ground is full of roots, dry and hard, just like in Vietnam," drawing shallow breaths and needing to sit as he told me. Flirtations with death attracted him. He was never afraid to take a risk, and his daredevil endeavors became family legend.

The idea of the vicarious nature of PTSD really rang true for me. It helped me understand the impact Peter's reaction to war had on the children and me. Even though we had not experienced his trauma directly, we lived with his anxiety afterward. And of course, for the children, this was throughout their entire lives. At least I had the advantage of growing to adulthood without this pressure. Studies of traumatized Vietnam veterans have revealed that the interconnectedness of families can result in spouses and children becoming excessively stressed. Proximity to anyone, happy or sad, affects us. As social beings, we adapt and react to the various situations we experience and to the people around us. Living with someone who is intense and touchy makes those around alert and reactive to mood changes. I identified strongly with this. The children and I were bound into Peter's needs, most especially for constraint and calmness.

With his anxiety levels already elevated, it became unbearable for him if we appeared to be out of control. Thus, around him we were cautious, conciliatory, and subdued. Not only Peter; now it also was apparent that our entire family had been affected by the trauma of war, and we had become collateral damage.

**AD—Month 2½.** *The great sadness of the demise of our family weighs on me. There were happy times. It was not all doom and gloom. There was a great deal of love. Overshadowed now by this dreadfulness.*

*Sadness also that a truly loving and gentle man could not surrender to those who loved him. He wanted to, he tried to, and there were times when we could think ourselves a content and normal family. But his pessimism dampened enthusiasm and frivolity. Living was serious. Yet inside lurked humor and lightness; I had seen it. Gone now. Gone forever. Leaving us the role of disentangling from his desperate despair, his anguished search for peace.*

As I began to unravel the relationship between Peter and me, and then with each of our children, the age-old impact of war emerged as a modern-day reality for our immediate family. The psychological damage of combat experiences has been apparent for centuries. There are endless stories of men and women who have returned home from any war morose, taciturn, overly sensitive to disorder, inflexible, and requiring stability. It is a theme that has been played out over and over since time immemorial. Now I began to look into my own life, and I could see how much of it had been adapted to ensuring that Peter had the constancy and tranquility that was essential to his survival. We, his wife and children, were essential props to his well-being. So, just as Peter's slow demise toward his unendurable torment began years before his death, so it had for each of us, as secondary sufferers of PTSD.

Uncovering this labyrinth of signs, symptoms, and causes of PTSD was helping me comprehend the enormous onslaught Peter had suffered, the despondency and defeat he must have felt with his post-combat dance of depression, desolation, and death. I no longer believe that Peter wanted to die. He wanted to ease his "aching heart." He did what he could to quell his anguish. The solution he chose was a drastic one. Over the top.

My horror and disbelief gave way to overwhelming compassion. I could see that even though there was a range of external situations that tipped the scales toward self-destruction, overwhelmingly it was escape from incessant inner agony that had become the catalyst. These scattered fragments became incorporated into my grieving.

# Chapter 5

## Grieving

Grief enveloped me. It swooped from above, dropped its web of entanglement and imprisoned me in its sticky restraint. Sabotaging everything, it greedily replaced any competitor. Numb for a long, long while, I became an observer of life, not a participant. To feel nothing was preferable to allowing that ravenous destruction a home.

Perhaps Peter had felt something of this—the fear that if you succumb to just the tiniest sensation, then the rest will force its cruel, unwelcome presence. It was too big. Gut-wrenching dejection.

I wanted to be alone. I wanted people around me. I didn't know what I wanted. Survival drove me. I had to keep going, to remain responsible, not to give in to the ghastliness. In the midst of Peter's turmoil, I had given up my own career, as he could not manage if I was far away or distracted. So I took over his business. I stepped into his shoes. I stepped into his being. If I became him, he wasn't gone. His anguish became mine. His sorrow wet my tears. He was everywhere. He was nowhere. Desperate despair.

*AD—Month 3. I feel his sadness. Surely, with treatment, he could have quieted his anxiety. Or perhaps the deep pit of darkness would never leave him. Is that what he felt?*

*I mouth the words, "He has suicided." I try them on and don't like the fit. I find it so hard to grasp as a reality. Difficult to feel the enormity. I imagine his body, decayed and rotten.*

*How can life have been so completely false? How could he keep his deepest, most significant feelings from me? Why couldn't he turn to me? Why didn't I know? It is as if we had nothing, yet I thought we had everything.*

*Where was he? Deep in his cocoon of sadness. How little I knew him, so alone in a world of openness. How alone he felt, with arms around him, supporting, giving, loving, and living; how alone he felt in his tortured mind that he could not hear the birdsong, smell the warm earth, accept love. How alone.*

*Now I am alone—cut down by that fatal blow. Betrayed. My life given as well as his.*

*AD—Month 3½. The grim reaper collects my mother.*

The trilogy. Father. Husband. Mother.
Numbness. Grieving is too painful. I don't want it.
It fluctuates. I have to wear it, that dunce's hat.
How could I ever recover? How could there ever be joy? My life was a sham. What had gone before had to be an illusion. I had lived

a dream. I had created a fantasy where my mate and I shared, where trust existed, where each whisper exchanged undying love. There could be no more certainty. The most secure of all, gone.

It was not just his absence I mourned; it was the unraveling of the delusion. What else had been fabricated? I longed to ask him, to discuss this huge event. But the one with whom I thought I shared had disappeared. My other half was missing. Like a grafted tree, I felt we had grown from the same trunk. Now severed, I swayed, wounded and weak. My rawness weeping.

Sequential, predictable emotions did not appear. A barrage of blandness occupied that position. The turbulence crept in when the sun was farthest, when the grip of night transported me to the precipice of torment. Dare I look over? *Move away*, I tell myself, *it is coming to capture you.* Tumbling. Tumbling into the unbearable horridness. I must wake. Trembling, misery overcomes me. *Breathe, slowly, deeply.* I must make this go away.

But I can't make it go away. It belongs to me, this sorrow.

Fitfully, I sight my adversary. It ebbs, it flows. It fluctuates, sometimes rapidly, often unexpectedly. Sometimes it is still; other times, it is persistent. At times direct; at others circuitous. I slip in and out of different emotions as their intensity and importance tumble over and around each other. And each peek at my enemy gives it form.

Mercilessly thrust into this unfamiliar territory, I do my best not to embrace it, not to feel the pain, not to become the victim. My life was transformed in one fell swoop. My despair is so great, I am frightened to give it full rein. My entire world has been altered dramatically. I had become widow and orphan within a few months. Palpable hurt and confusion surround me. My children, hurting, are devastatingly fatherless. It was almost more than I could bear.

Little wonder denial had the lead role in this drama. But other players—anger, guilt, sadness, desperation, and despondency—demanded the stage. Each shouting their words in case I miss the point.

The encore: deep, physical heartache.

Sabotaging the outside world, denying cruel facts, and creating one's own version eased distress:

*I just pretend he is away. It is the only way I can deal with it. I have his photos around and look at them, but I don't think he is dead. Just away.*

Lin

Each of us mourned differently, yet the same.

Anger was common. Confused anger. Anger twisted with love:

*I am so angry; if he weren't dead, I would kill him. Just the slightest thing goes wrong in my life, and I get so angry with him I shout at him as if he is just there. Mostly, I am angry with him for not being here, but I get angry too about what he has done to us all. Our family has been destroyed, and it will never be the same. How can anything be the same?*

Rowena

My own anger was slow to rise. On one level, I felt compassion for Peter; on another I felt deserted and incensed by injustice. It was difficult to place the understanding I now had of Peter's terrible torment alongside his choice of treatment. Especially when I watched people ravaged by disease desperately cling to the thing we call life. Indiscriminate.

I was acutely aware of the social prejudice that comes with suicide. Some of it formally endorsed.

**AD—Month 4.** *My mind torments me. When did "suicide" become a verb? It was a noun; now it is a verb—and a noun. Suicide. To commit suicide. He suicided. I say it in my mind, but I can't absorb it. They are just words.*

*Is it a crime? Will his soul ever rest? Some believe that he is condemned to eternal unrest. I find that distressing.*

My intrigue with terminology was influenced by the current trend to drop the word "committed" when speaking about suicide. Of course, this word implies a crime, which historically suicide was; in some places, it remains one. Almost universally, assisting suicide is a criminal act. In ancient times, suicide was considered self-murder and was declared both a felony against the state and a sin against God.

The departed cannot be prosecuted, so in their absence, it is the living who are condemned—and who do time.

These prejudices still exist. Insurance companies have not caught onto "trendy left" terminologies. Soft ideals don't make a profit. Financial burdens following the loss of a major breadwinner usually need to be addressed fairly quickly. That's why many of us take out life insurance. Even though Peter had taken out a life policy forty years prior to his death, his insurance company maintained that suicide voided the contract. With help, I fought and won, but I gained a direct lesson in culpability by association. There was no presumption of innocence for either Peter or me.

We weren't the only ones:

*I had to wait months before the insurance company paid up. They maintained that because it was suicide, it cancelled the insurance. I had to get legal help; after all, Mick had that policy for sixteen years. He took it out when he was an apprentice, scared he might get killed at work. What a joke that is. It made me feel sick and angry—and defenseless. I desperately needed the money for the mortgage, as his wage paid that, and I couldn't afford it by the time I fed the kids and other bills. It was so hard.*

Rowena

It was a hard lesson to learn that, just when social support was required, it was missing. What more practical way to demonstrate wrongdoing than to discriminate against families already in crisis. Such prejudicial judgments wore heavily on me and contributed to my feelings of isolation and injustice. It seemed that every way I turned I was greeted by denial and discrimination. Even when selling a house, if a suicide has occurred there, it must be declared to a potential buyer. Why not other types of death or drama? Messages of social disapproval abound. For instance, the media are discouraged from reporting graphic detail of suicide, supposedly to deter copycat suicides. This seems an irony in an era when an extraordinary array of information is available on the Internet. Inconsistent attitudes invade religious practices as well. Some religious factions still disallow eulogies as well as burial in the main part of the cemetery for anyone who has suicided. This is a carry-over from ancient times, when suicides were buried outside the city walls, and families were stripped of their assets and banished. Other religious orders lead the way with compassionate help for suicidal people and support for the bereaved. No wonder confusion, secrecy, and feelings of rejection are a big part of suicide grief.

These contradictory attitudes wove their negativity through my grieving. I was finding it difficult to acknowledge the horror of Peter's death to myself; now I felt I couldn't talk about it openly. The topic was tainted. Socially enforced silence.

Intertwined with the idea of suicide as a mortal sin is the portrayal of a restless soul in the afterlife. This theme emerges time and time again in classic and modern literature, religious or otherwise. Not allowed access to a place of eternal rest, the troubles of the dead are not over. Nor is closure available for the living, as Gina found out. Wide-eyed and speaking quietly, she explained her dilemma:

*I feel he is wandering the earth, a lost soul. It is his punishment, and he cannot pass over until he is truly sorry for what he has done. It might sound crazy, but it's what I believe.*

Gina

With suicide, even death can be denied.

Grieving the cause of death became as much a part of the grieving process as death alone. I was trapped in a stalemate. I became stuck at the point of death. When was this? Was it when his body died, or did it happen when his soul came to rest? Did he still suffer? Could he be released from this? Logic had little place in my anguished thoughts. Sometimes I thought I saw him at a distance. At other times, I agonized over his bodiless state. Where was his soul?

He could not exist as he had; he was no longer a conscious physical being.

Haunted by a violent and brutal death, Nicole and her family found their lives completely disrupted by her husband's suicide:

*It was a horror story, Charlie's death. We lived on a farm then, not a big one, and not far from town. So life was pretty good. We had suffered from the drought, but I worked at the local hospital as well, to make ends meet. Charlie grew up there, and maybe he had all that sadness of his parents trying to make it work; it must have been harsh in their time. But the kids were at the local school. You would think we were a normal, happy family. I always thought we were. Charlie kept himself to himself—you know the solitary, silent type. He loved the country, and he got heartbroken when it became dry and dusty. I don't know if that was the reason, although by then the drought had broken and things were starting to green up again. You know life's a cycle out there.*

*Anyway, just out of the blue, he took himself to the machinery shed and turned on the compactor. It crushed him. We didn't know. None of us knew where he was. Didn't even realize he was missing for most of the day. But he always liked his tea in the afternoon, and generally we were all home by then, so it was a good time to catch up as a family. We still didn't take much notice, as he sometimes would be down at the creek checking water levels, or riding the boundary checking the fences. But our son went into the shed to get something, can't remember what, and saw him, the machine still going. He realized straightaway his dad was dead and came out and got us. He could hardly walk and looked really pale. Suzie and I went in then. I rushed in, thinking I could save him, but he was a mess, blood everywhere, and his head squashed and broken like a watermelon. The images I still see of that. We were in such shock, feeling faint and not knowing what to do. My son called the police. It couldn't have been an accident because of the way he was. He had to deliberately get in the wrong place. Why? Why so awful? It was like he was trying to punish himself. I just don't understand.*

*We tried staying there. We closed the shed and never went in. But it didn't work. We were all too distraught. So we moved into town. The agent eventually sold the farm.*

*It has been really hard. Some people were extremely supportive. You know, country people are like that. But there were others who were cold and gossiped about us, like Charlie put a curse on everyone.*

Nicole

Eventually they moved from this town as well. They went to the city to be close to Nicole's family, where they could start life again.

I was having trouble myself. Like a fish caught in the shallows, I was floundering. I was trying desperately to return to familiar and safe waters, but I felt alienated from who I had been. Unsure of everything around me, I withdrew to try to calm the tempest within. Terrible gnawing ravaged my body, my mind, my entire being. There was no time frame, no predictable order—just a jumbled, crazy agony. Around me, my taken-for-granted world had vanished.

# Chapter 6

## Relationships

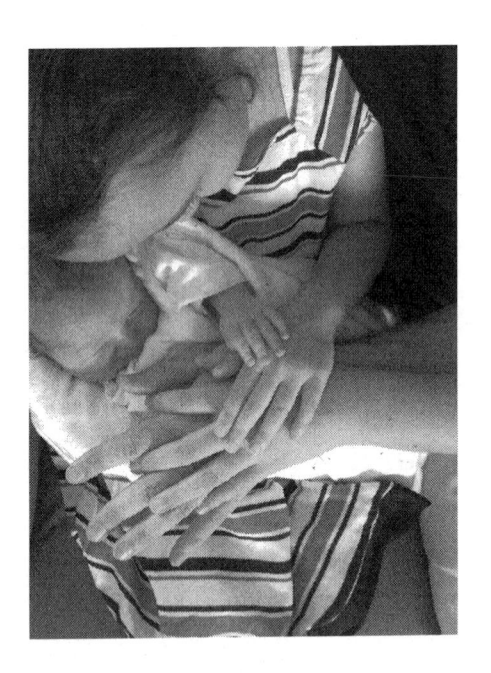

My grief infiltrated every relationship. Even a casual interaction was loaded with my guilt, my anxiety, my shame. I had learned to keep my secret early. I remember the look of alarm on the face of the roadside attendant who came to change my car tire when Peter was missing. "I ran into a gutter when I was driving in heavy rain, looking for my husband's body," I had told him truthfully as I stood alongside, clutching my umbrella. His hasty retreat was a clear signal that some information needs to be modified to protect other people's sensitivities.

I had stepped into a foreign place. My known world had dissolved, leaving only the knowledge that all is not as it appears, that life is transitory, and that absolute faith in anything is unrealistic. Uncertainty replaced confidence. Confidence that what I believed in would remain true, where life decisions were unquestioned, and where deep relationships were sound.

Everything was changing, including friendships. Some were strengthened. Others cracked wide open, revealing flimsy foundations. Initially, many people came out of the woodwork to express their shock and sympathy. Or their anger. Or their accusations. Now, alienation was creeping in. Some weren't able to cope with the continuing grief, strangeness, and sadness of my life. They seemed to be avoiding contamination.

A loyal band stuck with me. They became sounding boards in my quest for understanding, indulging my formidable grief with patience and compassion. These cherished connections sustained me—and continue to sustain me. As have similar relationships for other people:

*I could not have survived this without my closest friend. She has been wonderful, and I have been pretty rough on her. She got the brunt of all my anger and just took it without judging or complaining. But she is one of a kind. Nearly everyone else has disappeared. I have a new group of friends now. Many never knew me before.*

Carrie

I began to be selective with my relationships. My private anguish had become public property. What once had been the domain of a close family now had become the topic of e-mail news bulletins, hushed conversations, and even nasty letters. No copies to me. Curiosity without compassion can be harsh. Overly fascinated inquisitiveness satisfied the voyeuristic, content to keep me at a distance.

Without doubt, stigma had attached itself.

I identified with Rowena's tailored communication:

*I just don't talk about it anymore. I always say my husband is dead, but I never say, "He shot himself." You can tell. People look shocked and embarrassed. It's too uncomfortable.*

Rowena

Silent lament. Inside I was shattered. My self-perception had been crushed, and I was struggling with who I was. I felt differently about myself, and this influenced my relationships. Unintentionally, I was directing my grief to others. I was amazed that some people appeared not to value the relationships they had. I observed those with a compromised life and wondered at the randomness of life and death. I listened in disbelief to the insensitivity of jokes about suicide. I became jealous of those who appeared to have a relationship that seemed to be like the one I had lost. I was disturbed by inappropriate comments about suicide, and this jumble of feelings made it difficult for me to relate well to other people.

I suppressed my unease, silently watching, writhing inside with the unfairness of my new world. I had perfected modifying what I gave out. My thoughts constantly returned to questions that evaded resolution. My words were considered and controlled.

***AD—Month 4½.*** *I wake in the night and muse on relationships. I wonder what they are. Are they just what we perceive them to be? What is real, and what is just our imagination? Is everything only what we believe it to be? Are we bound to one another, or is there only ourselves, and is the rest just what we think it is?*

*Floating, removed from everyone, I hear, I see, but I do not feel. Who am I now? Is it a delusion to feel connected with anyone, to anything? Am I just my own self, alone?*

Peter had contemplated this. Toward the end of his life, he flipped from being the empathetic person I had known when he told me he now believed that "every man is an island." How difficult for me to embrace this philosophy. I could not accept that we arrive, live, and depart this world removed from others. The terrible impact of Peter's death demonstrated this more dramatically than he could have imagined. Yet he had felt so acutely alone that he believed his journey was solitary, even though our connection with others is absolutely essential to human existence.

We intertwine in all kinds of complex ways. Carole's secret relationship caused her great anxiety:

*Marty and I were lovers for years. I had given up the idea that he would leave his wife, like he had told me so many times. We worked together, and I was completely in love with him from the moment we met. He was exciting and romantic, and I gave my everything just to be with him whenever he could get away. It ended up being regular, and a few years ago, his wife came to see me. Can you imagine how I felt? She had found out and came to beg me not to see him anymore. They had kids and, you know how it is, family connections, schools and all that. I said I wouldn't see him anymore, but that only lasted a few weeks. He was everything to me. I don't have kids, and even though I was jealous of his family, I was happy to have what I could.*

*I found out about his death at work. Someone just said, "Marty's been found gassed in his car." I was gob-smacked. I was spinning. I felt faint. No way, it couldn't be. I just sat at my desk like a zombie, my head blank. I wanted to sink through the floor, to escape the chatter, everyone supposing this and supposing that. I think a few people were suspicious that we were having an affair, but I never told anyone, and I'm sure Marty wouldn't have.*

*I went to the funeral. Maybe I shouldn't have, but I couldn't help myself. It didn't seem suspicious, as a few people from work went. But I couldn't stop crying. I mean really sobbing. I was devastated.*

*I can't get over it. You know, move on. I am just stuck with it. The heartache. I told my friend, and she was angry with me. So I just say nothing now, but I'm heartbroken. I try to understand, but I can't. I'm not seeing anyone else. It's been over two years now since he died. I keep hearing that saying over and over in my head about how if you have to keep a relationship a secret, then you shouldn't be in it.*

*I get racked with guilt. You know, was it because of me? Why couldn't I help? But I'm dead jealous of his wife. She is at least a widow. I'm nothing. I went to his grave, and her name is on it, and his kids, but not mine. I don't exist.*

Carole

Relationships matter. They may be convoluted. They certainly change. Most profound was the change in my relationship with Peter. He had been the love of my life, yet he had left me. The one I trusted above all, the one with whom I shared my innermost feelings. Gone. I was gutted. With him went adoration. With him went intimacy. With him went joint parenthood. With him went companionship. And with him went faith in love.

What contribution had our relationship made to the eventual outcome of his death? Could it have been different? Hindsight provides more options than seem available at the time. Unfinished conversations. Underlying tensions. Fear of confrontation. Trying not to admit to the enormity.

The fairytale ended wrongly. Bewildered, powerless, and exhausted I had not wanted to accept suicide as a possibility.

Endless rationalization wasn't soothing my heartache.

Now I wanted to discuss this with him. But he was even more absent than he had been in life. His unspoken response was not unfamiliar. My relationship with him had begun in my head with his long absences and continued in a macabre way through internal, unanswered, dialogue. Yet we had been fundamentally entwined. Our relationship could not vanish instantly. I was reeling, lopsided by the removal of my counterbalance. I spun around, the mercurial nature of grief throwing obstacles in my way. Empathy, anger, complete abandonment. Hurling themselves at me. Randomly.

Profound changes, like Carrie:

*I felt like I was on a merry-go-round that was going faster and faster. Then, when he killed himself, I was thrown off. But I was used to the excitement and craziness of our lives. Everything stopped so suddenly, and then there was nothing. I couldn't let it go. I searched and searched for my life. I felt empty. I don't think I could have kept on the way we were, but I couldn't get used to it just disappearing either.*

Carrie

My awareness of Peter had altered; now my self-awareness was altering as well. I was no longer part of a couple, half of a whole. My first experience at being on my own with a group of couples had been confronting. At first, I wondered at the odd number of chairs at a dinner table. Who wasn't there? Silently I absorbed that Peter was missing. Now I was missing. The me I knew was not there either.

Tracey expressed this change:

*It is so weird. I mean, no one else in my group has had someone close die from suicide. They were all great to start off with, although, come to think of it, one guy was a bit strange, like he was angry with Joe. But after a while, I found I didn't fit in with that crowd anymore. It felt strange being with them, and I knew they felt strange too. I still see some of them on my own, but not as a group anymore.*

Tracey

Adjusting to being single was enormous for me. I had never lived alone. The house was hollow. Its walls whispered as I passed by, reaching out, greedily seeking the life that had sustained them, creating a home, not a vacated shell. My children, and theirs, returned to fill the void, to bring laughter and light where shadows encroached. Mutual support. And protection.

With the amour of my children around, I did not have to reach out. My self-confidence had been eroded, utterly. I felt abandoned, and the insecurity generated by these feelings transferred to other relationships. A pattern of self-sabotage and commitment phobia emerged where associations that were unlikely to succeed were chosen over ones that may have been more supportive. I was placing pressures on friendships that doomed them to failure. I set in place a cycle of unsatisfactory interactions that reinforced my negative perception of myself, my fear of rejection aborting a friendship before it could evolve into one that could hurt me. My sensitivity was so heightened that the slightest hint of rebuff sent me straight into my dark and solitary grotto, comforting in its familiar closeness.

Pressure on core relationships was taking its toll. We were all suffering, unable to make sense of our feelings. So much sadness. Sometimes dispersed horizontally. We each retreated, but emerged reformed and strengthened. Our closeness, insular and exclusive, wound into an impenetrable bond, an exclusive group withdrawn from outsiders.

Conversely, the dynamics of some relationships were strained to capacity. Feelings of blame, resentment, jealousy, and anger surged. Rather than forming a cohesive and supportive group, this tragedy placed pressure on a sense of unity and belonging. Fissures appeared. Negativity presided. Love was compromised.

I was not the only one to experience this. Sharon expressed the alienation she felt:

*After a while, his sister stopped contacting me. I didn't know why and rang and asked why. She said that it hurt too much because I reminded her that her brother was dead. She said that I should get on with my own life now. I wanted to shout at her and say, "But you are my life. You have been part of my life since we were teenagers, I can't just wipe it out." But I didn't. I didn't have the strength. I just pulled away, hurt.*

Sharon

It seemed that avoiding the terrible pain of grief and leveling it toward others was not unusual. Sometimes, a scapegoat was created, and misplaced anger found a target. Some relationships became destabilized and fractured. Entangled problems created confusion. Shared anxieties, guilt, shame, and sense of failure were often deflected to the person who had suicided. It seemed easier to blame the absent—and supposedly "deranged"—person than to look to collective concerns. The strong emotional impact intruded into various relationships, and suicide appeared to gain some kind of legitimacy.

Sadly it sometimes appeared as a solution to troubles. Tiffany struggled with the seduction of "ending it all":

*I was close to my sister and feel like she took me with her. She took pills, and I have some put away for when it's my turn. Maybe it's a family thing. I don't really know. But we were almost like twins, only a year apart, and she looked after me when I was little. It's like losing part of myself. Our dad's brother shot himself. A long time ago now, but it stays with you, that feeling that it's in your family. Then my sister. So much sadness…*

*I have no idea what my life is about. I do try, but I just get overwhelmed. I run out of energy, and the agony exhausts me.*

Tiffany

This sorrowful sentiment revealed the tendency of a suicidal identity to cluster in families. This predisposition, just like other problems, seems to combine elements of our natural inheritance with what we experience through life; the intertwining of nature with nurture.

One story of domino suicides within a family was a poignant reminder of the powerful connections of relationships. Contagious nightmare. Relationships bound so tightly that knock-on suicides assumed a frightening validity. Interwoven to the point of death.

All my relationships were changing. Even my relationship with suicide was different. It now had its own identity. I needed to avoid the intensity of my own feelings just to endure this appalling beast. Like Peter, I learned to keep the depth of my feelings secret. I hid them in the file of my subconscious, thinking them safe. They were subdued for a while but in danger of emerging randomly, indiscriminately, and forcibly. From this precarious platform I stepped into the turmoil of personal chaos.

# Chapter 7

# Chaos

As I wrestled with the intimacy of suicide, its peculiarity took its toll. Alliance with the bizarre removed me from what is considered normal. I felt alienated from everyday interactions and struggled to maintain my sense of self-worth. I was swallowed up by chaos; everything around me seemed unfamiliar. I lost sight of all I had assumed was trustworthy and was unable to find a footing in the shifting uncertainties of my daily life.

*AD—Month 6.* *I gasp for air, frightened all will disappear. I am terrified. I don't know what is real and what is not. I reach for familiarity, but it is not there. Only fear, only the unknown. I am living as an automatic being without conscious direction. I try to find myself, but I am lost.*

*I am dragged into the spiral: down, down, down. Let me breathe. Why so black? Why so dark? Why so final? Why THAT choice?*

*Around are voices, and faces, but they are not real; they do not engage. They are an illusion. I am lost.*

My known world had disappeared, and in its place were feelings and thoughts I did not recognize. I replayed the tragedy of his death, struggling to come to terms with it as a reality, hoping the outcome could be different. I wondered why others were concerned with outwardly trivial matters that I found of little significance.

The complexities around suicide didn't just go away. They seemed too strange and too big to deal with. How Peter had died was harder to accept than his death. It was overshadowed by violence, police involvement, the postmortem, the coroner's report, blame, stigma, and secrecy. Out of the realm of the majority. Rowena told me that she felt bizarre and isolated:

*I remember the day I received the coroner's report. It came in the mail, and I sat on the step reading it as if it had nothing to do with me. It described my husband's body, what bits weighed, and how it looked. And that they concluded he had committed suicide.*

*I was at the school picking up the kids later that day, and I couldn't believe that everyone was just chatting like nothing had happened. I found it impossible to talk to anyone. I mean, how do I start off the conversation, "Hello, I've just been reading my husband's autopsy report and the descriptions of how his brain and skull were half gone"? You just can't. I felt frightened and sick, and I needed to rush home and hide.*

Rowena

Battling with horrendous realities while simultaneously living in a world where such things are alien to many people made my emotions swing wildly. I felt as if I had been thrown into a massive tidal wave with nothing to cling to. My feelings were all over the place, as frothy as the spume and spray. I lurched from compassion for Peter to anger; relief that he was dead; overwhelming horror at his actions; intense hurt at what I perceived was betrayal; crushing sadness; the desire to move on; and disbelief that any of this had happened. Others were just as confused:

*My head was unable to take stuff in. It really was like sleepwalking or being on drugs. I would try to do something, but my feet would disappear from under me. I just couldn't get it together. I hate to think what I was like at work. I would forget what I was talking about mid-sentence and have to change what I was saying. I don't know if anyone noticed, but I would just go completely blank, and that's pretty scary. I am much better now, but if I get pressured I am frightened that it will happen again.*

Carrie

It seemed impossible to find structure within this chaos. A perpetually changing medley of emotions made it difficult for me to sort through my grief. I could not comprehend how I could ever find stability again when everything familiar had vanished. I had lost confidence in my ability to understand anything.

I felt that I no longer knew myself, since I had so badly misjudged the person closest of all.

My turmoil extended to practicalities. I found it almost impossible to manage my daily affairs, let alone complex administrative and business matters. All around me was emotional, financial, and physical chaos. Some of it was an indication of what was happening in Peter's mind. Again, Carrie had similar feelings:

*It has taken me years to really go through everything. I threw away a lot in the beginning, like clothes, but there was so much other stuff. It seemed like the messier his mind got, the messier his things became.*

Carrie

A peculiar mix of order and disarray surrounded me. I could see that Peter had struggled to maintain an appearance of control; yet, as I sorted through the debris of his life, I began to see hidden disorder. Despite the fact that he had a successful business, it became apparent that, for some time before his death, Peter had been suffering from jumbled thoughts. The fine line between his extraordinary talent and the weight of his tormented soul became apparent.

So much needed to be organized. Decisions needed to be made. I lacked energy and clarity. The slightest thing seemed momentous. Drought, recession, and employment issues were daily realities. Somehow, the business kept going, but additional responsibilities were a burden. I became emotionally and physically burned out. Unable to remove myself from a downward spiral of despair, I became exhausted by loneliness, unresolved grief, depression, and an inability to accept how Peter had died.

I had absorbed his anxieties myself, transferring and accepting the chaos. I became expert at targeting the essential and discarding the surplus. Papers piled on my desk. Bills, notices, letters. Some required action. I tried several systems, frighteningly aware of the dire consequences of defaulting on a loan. Major financial decisions were emergency responses that I tried to consider calmly, but my choices were based on immediate survival needs for me and for my family. Each day was a triumph if we could all stay alive.

My frenzy was directed to an obsessive concern for my children. They in turn were concerned for me. They were the ones who shared my sorrow, saw my tears, and shed their own. We were devastated and stumbled around in desperate confusion.

**AD—Month 7.** *Images of my clutch, my chickens under my wing, dart in and out of my mind's eye. Often on our own, our special bond* *formed long ago. Fear of disaster well practiced. A bomb blast in Rhodesia as it transitioned to Zimbabwe. Announced on the radio. Mother and children huddled around. Dad is there. Could he be hurt? No one knows. United then in alarm, united still in painful bewilderment.*

Life was happening around me. One son's marriage was dissolving while the other's was unfolding. My daughter moving home, divorced, with little ones. Change and more change. Spinning. Grasping at mirages. Faster and faster. Fearful for their unhappiness. Frightened that they, too, could fall into the void of oblivion. Suicide had become a reality. Perhaps it could soothe the chaos.

Tiffany's reference to her own bleakness was disturbing:

*It feels so heavy, everything around me. My head feels tight. At times, I have to take painkillers, strong ones, just to be able to do normal things. I have lost my job. My boss kept pressuring me. Said I didn't get there on time and I was too disorganized. I tried to get another job, but it's too hard. I don't do much now, and, you know, I have thought so often of just how I could end it all.*

Tiffany

The mercurial nature of grief had taken on a different dimension. It had assumed the cloak of Death. The dark unknown became attractive, like Sirens to sailors, luring body and soul to the underworld.

Sharon told me how she had slipped into the depths of despair:

*I did feel like suicide. I couldn't see a way out of where I was. So alone and so disillusioned. My whole life, it was my whole life, gone. I couldn't bear it.*

*I was living in a sort of dream, and it just went crazy. I was kind of numb for ages, but as the feeling started, it was beyond me. I saw his face, haunting me. Not blank but menacing, almost dragging me to him like a magnet. He was so much part of me, of who I was, I couldn't be free of him. I couldn't let the pain go. It ate into me, like a poison or acid or something evil. I wasn't doing well at home. It had just been us since the kids left, and he was in every corner of the house. I couldn't use the front door anymore and had to come in through the kitchen. Pretty awkward with groceries, especially if it was raining. I slipped on the stairs one time and just lay there like a log, the rain dripping on me from the porch roof. It was as if I had run out of living. I watched as a tin rolled down the steps and didn't care. It was where I felt I had come to the bottom, broken, with no energy to get up.*

*But I did. Maybe the rain sobered me. I struggled onto my knees and crawled to the door, leaning on it as I got up to open it. I sat at the table, wet and cold, and thought that I had reached the end of the road. Not even sure how I pulled myself out, but I made some tea and had a hot bath. I thought of slipping under the water. I even tried it to feel how easy it was. But I couldn't do it. Sort of snapped me out, that terrible gasping for breath. I guess that was my lowest ebb. The feelings of killing myself gradually went away. I think it might have been because I really did try it, sort of, well I thought of it at least, but I really didn't want to die.*

*My daughter found a counselor for me, and I still go. She has helped me. Just talking about it and finding a way I can understand how I feel. A friend suggested I go when Jack died, but I saw my doctor and got some pills, you know, anti-depressants. They probably helped, but I was really in a dream state.*

Sharon

Desolate moments for Tiffany and Sharon. My thoughts were not so dark, but no matter how hard I tried, I could not get on top of my life. I managed a daily routine. I was going to work each day. His work. Nevertheless, it offered a sanctuary where I could hide, hoping the dreadfulness would wash over me.

Yet I was consumed by guilt. I felt Peter's death was a public burden, exposing many people to this ghastly brutality, and I thought that I was responsible for their pain. It kept me away from mine. I could not look at my own grief. I could not help my own children.

I had picked up Peter's baton of despair and was running with it, as directionless as he had been.

I was still shocked. I couldn't feel. Adrenaline addict.

Around me was the complicated clutter of his life. Much he had kept hidden. I sorted through paperwork, his personal things, an overflowing garage, his problematic business. As I unraveled and discarded, I felt voyeuristic. I was pulling his life apart and examining each minute part, trying to work out what role it had played. The veneer was organized, shielding disarray. Symbolic of the Peter emerging in my mind, the Peter I didn't know, tucked safely in the drawers and cupboards of his past. Falling from a book, a note written long ago. Absolute evidence that he had carried his troubles a long way. Eating into him, the nightmares he tried to keep at bay by placing a pillow over his head. Prolonged torture.

Perhaps this intricate inspection was necessary. Perhaps it helped me see through his eyes, helped me feel some of his pain, helped me reinvent the person I had so readily seen as whole white light. Dazzled by the brilliance. Now my own refracting prism was dispersing this to its color components. The rainbow aftermath of a weeping sky.

For all my anger, hurt, confusion, I cared for him still.

Then I began clearing out the house. I needed him scrubbed from my life. If he had gone, I would make sure he went entirely. Not just rubbish bins full but commercial waste bins in the driveway to take away his life. The garden, too, needed trees removed and new ones planted. Nothing would be the same.

Yet he lingered. In my heart. I could not cover his life with a new coat of paint. I could not remove his terrible pain. I had to take it on. I had to feel it for him, to ease his burden. I had to help him find peace. Illusive. Unseen. Unreachable peace.

It escaped me.

I lurched from one chaotic moment to another. In vain, I tried to find direction. As I was dragged into this emotional turmoil, other aspects of my life went askew. The protracted psychological barrage was detrimentally influencing my physical health.

# Chapter 8

# Living

***AD—Year 2.*** *I feel sick. I am struggling to stay alive. How can I sleep so much? My body aches. I can hardly keep my eyes open.*

*They take my blood. I am sweating. I feel sick. I feel faint. Hospital? No, I don't think so. Too noisy. Too much activity. Not nurturing. I would rather be lost on my own. I want to sleep. And sleep.*

*It must be days that I slept. Fitfully. Wakened only by the dog. Faithful. Sleeping too. Snuggled into my body. I care, she says. I am here.*

I had been caught unaware. I didn't expect my body to fail me at my time of greatest need. Apart from the constant feeling of nausea, I had thought I was physically strong. But the relentless weight of grief was wearing me down, and eventually, my body, which had valiantly strived to support me, gave in.

I had been living in an emotional limbo, my wretchedness frozen like an overloaded computer with too much information to process. It seemed as if my suppressed emotional responses were locked inside my physical body. Screaming to be released yet transfixed at the same time. Too immense to contemplate, they were invisibly knotted inside.

Eventually I became physically unwell. Far easier to identify and treat than heartache. There also was a sense of immediacy, an acuteness that prompted action. Prolonged sadness had made me susceptible to common illnesses that normally I would have been able to resist.

I didn't know how to protect myself from this new vulnerability. Neither, it appeared, did others. Nellie appeared to be floundering:

*Thinking you'll get over something like this is so wrong. I mean, people think you'll get over it, but you can't. My friends have tried to help me, they really have, but I'm sort of trapped. I guess it's who I am now. I can't forget the memory of finding him like that. It drives me crazy. I feel sick all the time. I have tried. I really have tried, but I can't stop the memories. So I drink. Maybe that helps. I dunno. But it's feeling sick all the time that wears me down. It doesn't stop.*

Nellie

I was completely out of my comfort zone as well. I lacked the ability to change my usual methods of survival and blundered on inappropriately and ineffectively. My depleted resources were only just enough to keep me alive. The extra effort required for more than just basic living wasn't available to me.

Evan's coping mechanisms weren't helping him much either:

*The thing I noticed the most was that I kept eating. It seemed to settle the uneasiness in my stomach. But at the same time, I did less and less. I became addicted to the sports channel and would have a beer or two, then eat whatever I could: chips and pies, that kind of thing. I used to play sports once, not watch it. I knew I was eating myself to bad health, but I couldn't stop. I didn't go to the doctor until I felt real bad. My blood pressure was high, and it hadn't been before. I had some kind of a thing that was like a heart attack, but it wasn't. I ended up in emergency. Until then, I hadn't taken any notice of my doctor or taken care of myself. I'm still not real well. I belong to a gym now, and I try to go, but most of the time I don't have the energy.*

Evan

The relationship among suicide, stress, and illness differed for us all. For some, it spiraled out of control:

*I didn't connect any of it to Tina's disappearance for a long time. I was always sick, with flu and things like that. Like I just had no resistance to anything. Then I got really sick and had to take three months off work. The doctor said it was a type of virus and did all sorts of tests. I just felt unwell, no energy, and although I am back at work now and much better than I was, I never feel completely well.*

*Then Bill [Petra's husband] got cancer. Why does everything happen to one family? He didn't seem to react that much to her disappearance. In fact, he hardly said a thing. He got angry in the beginning, and I was frightened that he would really lay into her when she came back. But of course she never did, and we just stopped talking about her. We just got on with our routine, going to work, coming home, eating, and that, but we never mentioned her. And we went on like that for ages. He didn't eat that well. Lost his appetite. Then he used to get indigestion and just feel uncomfortable. I persuaded him to see the doctor. Then, after some tests, they discovered he had stomach cancer. What a shock!*

*He had surgery and has had to change his diet. But he is okay now; he didn't need chemo or anything, but there's a lot he can't eat, and a lot he didn't eat that he has to now, like fruit and such. In some ways, it has probably done him good because if it had gone on, who knows?*

*And my son hasn't been well either. He took to drugs and acting out. That has been a serious problem for us. I'm not sure how much we can take.*

Petra

It was impossible to quantify how much suicide affected each one of us. Without doubt, my children and I were deeply wounded. We were emotionally and physically fatigued. One by one, we succumbed to major health problems that hit like sledgehammers. It seemed none of us, like Carole, was free of the enormous weight of shock and sadness:

*It's an all-over thing. I feel like I've aged at least ten years. Well, hard to put a figure on it really, but I feel old, older than my age. I'm forty-one, but I feel like I'm sixty. My joints have seized up, and I hardly have any energy, and my hair has thinned, and it's starting to go gray. I ache everywhere. I was tested by the doctor, and he told me that I have a problem with my blood sugar, it's like a pre-diabetes thing. I guess I'm just old before my time. I'm sure it's the stress. Mind you, I think I've coped pretty well, on a practical level anyway, but it's like something had to give, and I guess it's my health.*

Carole

It seemed as if suicide was the ultimate demonstration of the invisible strands that connect us internally, within ourselves, and externally, with others. Without this fusion, I would be inanimate and pain-free. Peter's sadness would have no effect on me. It was not like that. So interwoven, so connected, that I felt myself half dead. Physically depleted, I pushed myself to stay alive.

My experience was not unique. Tammy's illness was lengthy and severely debilitating:

*About three years later, I had an acute sickness. I felt really low, no energy, and I literally collapsed. One morning, I fell on the floor and just couldn't get up. I pulled myself across to get my mobile and called my sister. She was getting ready for work, and even though she lives a* few hours' drive from my old flat, she dropped everything and came and drove me to hospital. I stayed there for several days while they did tests. My temperature was up, and they were worried. My joints were aching, too. I was pretty spaced out. They couldn't find anything, just a virus, they said. Anyway, they gave me some antibiotics and said I could go home. When my sister picked me up, she thought I looked terrible and took me back to her place. She is married, and they have two beautiful kids. They've got a nice little house, and she made me a bed on the back verandah. It's closed in and cozy.

I stayed there two years! Can you believe that? It just sort of happened. We thought it would be a day or two, but I just sort of went into complete shutdown. After a while, we realized that I needed to give up my flat. I took sick leave from work to start off with, so I paid the rent for a bit. But when I didn't come back, my boss said it was better if I resigned. He was actually pretty nice about it, but the bottom line was I had no money coming in. My brother-in-law packed up my flat and put most of it in their garage, I couldn't afford storage. I went to my doctor and got a certificate so I could get assistance. I spent all that on pills. I tried everything recommended. Quite frankly, I don't think she had a clue. After a while, I changed doctors. The new doctor talked about diet and was sympathetic, but neither of them connected it with the suicide. Now, when I think about it, it seems so obvious that that's how it started.

Anyway, we just carried on. Me sleeping a lot and trying all different treatments. My poor sister. She worked and had her little boy in care during the day and her daughter was at school. I couldn't even help much with them. I babysat occasionally, but not much. And my forever-patient brother-in-law. I suppose there were times when it must have been too much for them, but they didn't take it out on me. It was like I needed time out from living. I didn't get worse, but then I didn't get better, either. The worst part was my aching joints and just feeling exhausted from nothing.

It took forever before I started to get some life back into me. A little bit at a time I stayed up longer and was able to help a bit. I wanted to *do yoga but didn't have anywhere near the energy. My sister ordered some meditation and yoga CDs, and I started that way. I slowly built up to a gentle type of yoga at home.*

*I still don't have energy like I used to, but I have managed to find work. Much slower. I work with animals now. I do reception at a rescue place. It's quite different from my old corporate life, but I like it. The people are more caring, and the animals are mostly adorable. So I have a new flat and a new life. Not full on. I'm still slow and reserved. I'm just walking distance from my sister now. I can't imagine what it would have been like without her.*

Tammy

In different ways, each of us found that the stress of suicide challenged the subtle balance of our lives. I felt swamped by the suicide tsunami and found it difficult to comprehend that the forcefulness could ever subside. I couldn't tolerate being constantly tossed about. I needed to sit with my pain and let the wave wash over me. I needed the stillness and silence of seclusion, at least for a while. I needed to smooth the transition into my radically different life. I felt I had to do this alone and sought sanctuary in isolation.

# Chapter 9

# Sanctum

Not only did I feel disconnected from other people, I also felt disconnected from myself. I was unable to absorb the range of reactions I was experiencing, and, being unable to share these openly, I withdrew to my own company. Isolation was intoxicating. I felt that no one could understand the depth of my despair. I found everyday conversation banal. Without doubt, retreating was a reprieve from what felt like the empty clatter of other people's lives. I needed the sanctuary of quietness and tranquility. I quarantined myself from the outside world.

Peter's suicide had challenged my most fundamental values. I questioned the meaning of life. I wondered about life after death. What did the sanctity of life mean? Would Peter ever find peace or was he condemned forever for taking his own life? Or is everything an illusion, a projection of our great imagination? These questions teased urgently, demanding my involvement.

***AD—Year 3.*** *Right to the core. Into my soul—whatever and wherever that is. I don't really know, but the ache is unreachable—deep, squeezing the essence of who I am. Greedy for life—beyond my body, my feelings.*

*I retreat. To interact is too much. The day-to-day stuff is too hard. I need stillness. I need to be alone.*

*The garden embraces me. Here, anxiety can be quieted. Life and death are living side by side—the cycle of nature, a silent connection with the world, the universe, eternity. It is an escape from the bustle and noise of living. It soothes. It heals. Its demands are quiet. In this place, I can allow change from within, like an insect metamorphosing. This pain needs stillness to calm.*

Little seemed to matter in daily life. It would all disappear, in any case. The transience of life. Impermanent. Incorporeal. I could no longer touch or feel it. Numb to life, it continued around me.

Mia's story of her husband's suicide jolted me from my introspection:

*It was like an act of terrorism where the innocent are bombed. It was so violent. Alex had been controlling, and it was like an extension of his personality, a really extreme version. We disintegrated as a family. People blaming each other, angry, shocked, sad, all those emotions thrown into a cauldron and boiling over. I moved away immediately. There was no way I could live in that house anymore. Why is it that people think it's okay to kill themselves where every day is a reminder of what happened? I guess they don't think. That's the point isn't it?*

*My son has rented the house out, and one day, I will sell it. I don't see my son so often anymore. He got married, and they have moved to another town. Anyway, after my husband's suicide, there was a lot of strain between us. He was angry with me. He felt that, if I had been a better wife to his father, this never would have happened. But he doesn't understand. His father was dominating and controlling—to me, not to our son. Strange isn't it? You often hear of children suffering from an abusive father, but my son was cherished by his father. Maybe that's the problem; he feels that I took his father away. But you know, I didn't. Our son had left home, and my husband became more and more difficult to live with. I had always been very attentive, as I was brought up in an old-fashioned way, where women looked after their men. So my son's attitude really hurts. But what can I do? I hope that, one day, he will understand, but I have to stop thinking about it. He is to be a father himself soon, and I hang onto the hope that this will make him realize how much parents love their children.*

*The emotional stuff is the hardest to deal with. I went to a retreat for a while, and I've learned to meditate. I think about it a lot, suicide I mean. It's so hard to understand when you don't feel like that, but I think I have learned to accept it as part of life. I mean, you hear about it all the time. I hadn't had any experience of a close death, so it made me start thinking about the big issues. Maybe we're removed from it these days. Years ago, kids died, and there was more war, and terrible diseases that wiped out lots of people. I guess death was more usual. Or early death I mean. We expect people to live long lives these days. So it's confronting when someone chooses not to live.*

*We never think about our own deaths. Well, I hadn't. I do now. I'm more philosophical about it. I sort of realize it's the pattern of life. We live and then we die.*

Mia

Like Mia, I needed space for reflection and reframing my beliefs. Inevitably, we all die. The unknown is when and how. Peter had confronted this mystery. He had taken it on and written his own exit. He had controlled the uncontrollable. He had solved the secret for himself.

> **AD—Year 4.** *Still feeling sensitive. Brash, loudness, too much. My soul weeps—for humanity. For cruelty. It seeks softness and beauty. It is shy, and I search in vain.*
>
> *Time and again, I am thrust back to my solitary musings. I read only morose mutterings of forlorn and lost lives. Humor or light fiction are of no interest. I busy myself with my nest, trying to keep away intrusion and aggression.*
>
> *I desperately pursue calmness—a mythical place where hurts are soothed, where universal comfort can be found, where betrayal does not exist. Its emptiness crowing.*

Searching for any small relief, any stillness within; I read many books, hoping to find a clue, an ally, to nod knowingly, to illuminate the darkness. Heart-wrenching music is a soul mate, connecting me with humanity and the agelessness of human suffering:

> *I have found music a great help. Somehow, music, especially some classical pieces, touches my feelings and expresses what can't be said with words. I can really let my emotions out. I hide in my hole and play deep music. It might not seem that healthy, but it really does make me feel better. Well sad, then better.*
>
> Sharon

Without doubt, suicide had wrenched open a cavern of discontent. My deepest feelings had been reached by a penetrating sorrow. My grief became a *momento mori*, a reminder that I, too, will die.

I sat with these troubles and absorbed them into my very being. Even the tragic events I was exposed to daily through the media did not provide immunity from the reality of my own heartbreak. The distance could not be traversed from the television screen, or the printed word, into my own life. This wretchedness appeared to be mine alone.

Bleakness struck. I had been exposed to the precariousness of life. My life had changed forever while it appeared that many people around me were immune to this weightiness. Unable to face a noisy and hurried world, I was subdued by a mantle of melancholia. Like Tracey, I needed to retreat:

*I regularly stay in bed all day. I read or sleep. I do it on the weekend, when I'm not at work and when I know all my friends are with their partners. I guess I could socialize with them, but I'm the only one on my own, and I have to force myself to be chatty or pretend that I'm having fun. I wasn't like this before Joe's death.*

Tracey

Withdrawing from the hurly-burly of life, embracing a lonely serenity, and removing myself from the insistence of the tumultuous surging tsunami of despair was addictive. The depths of isolation were seductive. However, to remain was debilitating. A slow consumption of life. Having met the gloom of pessimism, I wanted to replace it with lighter feelings.

Yet, I didn't know how to release myself from this self-imposed exile. I didn't know where I could go. I didn't know what I could do. I didn't even know if I really wanted to.

Medication and counseling had no appeal for me. They couldn't fill the void of loneliness and grief. I had been to a counselor, briefly, early in my story. Now I needed someone with the sensitivity to travel with me and to provide me with the means to negotiate my arduous journey. For a time, my need remained unmet. I found comfort from gentle interactions, not ones that were confronting.

My resistance was partly due to the overt confirmation that I was depressed if I saw a counselor. After all, I felt that it was Peter who had had a problem, not me. Looking deeply into my own distress might reveal that I was profoundly entwined in Peter's anxieties and that the contagious nature of his psychological pain remained with me. I was not ready to look at, or accept, my own despair.

It seemed shameful to be depressed. Years of living with Peter's emotional anguish had taken its toll. I had learned to accommodate and adapt to the pressures of uncertainty and a disturbed relationship. Keeping my emotions hidden had become my normality. Now I needed to unravel this. Others were not as stuck as I appeared to be:

*I still see my counselor, five years later. I hate it, as every time I go, I am reminded that I have a problem, but then when I do go, I feel better. Sometimes I skip it for months, and other times I can't afford it. I tend not to go when I feel that I'm on top of everything, when my life seems to be working out, and the times when I almost feel normal. But I can't always manage on my own, and my counselor encourages me to face the things that worry me. She helps me look at lots of things that I prefer to ignore, but basically she does help.*

Carrie

Processing grief fluctuated for each of us. Some were able to monitor their emotional status relatively easily; others were taken by surprise by the depth of emotion prompted by particular situations. Tammy described how complex this was for her:

*More than anything, it's a feeling that no one else can have any idea of how I feel. I am tortured by how he did it and if he's at peace. I see it endlessly in my head. It was so gross. He had been in the car for four days, and the smell was unbelievable. I had been at my sister's, so he had planned to do it while I was away. I didn't put my car in the garage straight away, so I came inside first. He should have been at work so I didn't even realize at first. But then there were odd things, like messages on the phone not checked and mail and papers not brought in. It just felt strange. When I found him, I so freaked. I opened the door of the car and just vomited. It was disgusting.*

*I wonder about life after death and if he is in heaven or hell. I am a Christian, and I find it hard to forgive him. My counselor said I* should, but killing yourself is a crime. Well, I think it is, and I just can't come to terms with it. Is he wandering in some place between worlds? I don't know.

I wonder how you get over this kind of thing. I went away with a friend for a holiday not long after. I carried on for a few years, living on my own, and now I'm back on my own after being with my sister for so long. I'm getting used to being by myself. My sister helped me clean up the car. Then my brother-in-law sold it for me. I had to move out after I got sick, and I've bought my own flat now. I don't have to see or smell the garage anymore. When I'm in my flat it's like I can lock everything I don't like outside.

Tammy

There is a spiritual dimension to seeking solitude, an intimate personal quest for inner peace that requires privacy. Generally, there is little public sympathy to the heartache of death beyond a few weeks. Without any external indication that someone is grieving, others are not aware of their immense sorrow. Overt signs, such as black armbands worn at funerals, torn clothing, and widow's weeds, have gone out of fashion. And a longer grieving period, once indicated by the traditional wearing of black or muted colors with little or no jewelry for a year, defined the status of a widow in particular. Re-emerging into society was a slow process and was signified by the gradual wearing of less-somber clothing; conversely, continuing to wear dark clothing demonstrated an unhealed wound.

These forms of acknowledgement seem kinder than the individual stoicism we expect nowadays. Lack of public awareness forced me to create my own sanctuary. I needed to be resilient to participate in the external world, and often it was difficult to find the capacity for this. I was trying to accept my hurt. I took it in intermittently by slow absorption. Piece by tiny piece, I began a cautious reconnection with others.

# Chapter 10

## Resilience

There came a time when, despite the seemingly endless agony, I chose more than survival. I chose Life. I had been consumed by grief, but from deep within, the will to go on living the best I could drove me from my place of hiding. I started by peeling back the layers to see who I had been, so I could know who I was now.

This didn't happen in a defined or formal way. Changes wove through my life as I constantly adapted to the confrontations Peter's death had thrown at me. I learned to be kinder to myself. I had been my own worst critic, accepting blame and guilt, before I began to realize that I was just part of a story, not its creator.

Tentatively, I embraced compassion, for myself as well as for Peter.

**AD—Year 4½.** *It plays in my mind like an old movie. I am transfixed by the overture, repeating, repeating, repeating the opening line, "he suicided"; trying to imprint that thought, the awful knowledge that this story is not the predicted one, not the one that unfolds as expected. It is the terror of the nightmare come to claim naïveté, contentment, joy, and love. It is the black shadow of fear, loneliness, hopelessness, and despair.*

*While he lives in my mind, the man I dreamed, this reality has no place. He was not there, only Death, only sadness, only desperation.*

*I must look into this void to see the shape of blackness, to walk in it and feel its coldness pressing around me, teasing for entrance, seeking refuge in the living. Can it steal my flesh with its insatiable appetite? Must it consume all?*

*Had I the strength to refute its hazy emptiness, I could mock its presence. But it stole from me the mold that formed my being. Need I now become unformed to reform, to reinvent my perceptions of reality, of who I am, of who he was?*

*I have to escape this devouring nightmare.*

How was I to do this? Could I just say to my dark moments, "Go away. I don't want you." Well, that was a start, but the complex base to life's most perplexing puzzle, its meaning, required a lot more than asking it to remove itself. If there was no meaning to life, it would be intolerable, impossible to endure. The meaning, it seemed to me, was Life itself. Not life, but Life. A paradox. "Life" gave reason to living.

I wondered where it came from, this spark. This will to live. This tiny breath, this beginning. This renewal that dwelt within. Despite all. Despite the dreary no-man's land of nothingness. Despite the bleakness. I wanted to go on. Succumbing to gloom was horror upon horror. I no longer wanted to satisfy the greed of the voracious void of emptiness.

Endless philosophies, religions, and fables relate this capacity for survival. Human suffering, some say, is necessary for true compassion. For many, that compassion begins for oneself. Joanne's will to survive came from an understanding of her changed life:

> *I can't really describe to you how affected I've been. I couldn't erase it from my mind. I went to counselors and took anti-depressants, but in the end, I just realized that it had become part of who I am. I was really struggling to get back to how I'd been, to be who I was, but I had changed. I am changed. Realizing that was a turning point. I wasn't that happy about it, as I've changed a lot, but somehow, I began to feel more content. I don't fight it anymore. I didn't do a whole lot of soul searching, although I did go over lots of stuff with the counselor. It was something that just dawned on me one day, like, "Hello, I feel like I'm a different person. Well, hello, you are."*
>
> Joanne

My innermost feelings were constantly changing. There was no epiphany where I became enlightened. It was more like an ember after a fire has died down, where warmth remains. A tiny, fragile hint that, given oxygen and fresh fuel, a fire could burn again. There was no bonfire, nowhere to place a match and begin a raging furnace. There was just a glimmer of life to be fanned and encouraged.

I didn't set out to reinvent myself. I merely went on living the best I could. I absorbed changes without dissecting and analyzing them too much. I didn't have the defined intention of creating a new identity. Subtly, over a period of time, life force breathed itself back into my being.

The changes in Lisa's life weren't structured either:

> *My attitude to everything has changed. I don't quite know how it happened; it just sort of did. Since that terrible day, I thought life could*

never be good again. It was so shocking. I have been to hell and back again. And watching my mother, God, that's been awful. But you know, Michael was a wild kid, and he certainly had his problems. At least they're over now. But it was still impossible to believe that he had really done it. My other brother's been out of control since, poor Mum. I had to back off from them all. Dad left years ago, and I don't see him much anyway. But I've just had to do my own thing. My partner's great; he's really supportive. But it did take me a long time to feel even half good.

I haven't done anything in particular, just thought about it a lot. That's how I've changed. I think differently. I feel more sorry for people, and I am much quieter. It's okay though; I don't mind.

Lisa

Others were taking ownership of their story:

It was hard to find the energy to do new things, but stuff about my life didn't interest me anymore. I just let it all go for a long time. I've never been that much of a social person anyway. I sold our house. People told me not to, that I shouldn't make such a big change straight away. But how could I keep living there? I don't regret it. I have a townhouse now, and it's quite comfortable. There's a little garden and a leafy outlook, as it's next to a park. It's really nurturing being there. I've got a cat, and she's good company. I read a lot and sit in the sun when I can. I'm not much of a gardener, but I enjoy being outside. My big indulgence is having a beauty treatment once a month. It makes me feel rejuvenated, and I usually meet a friend for coffee after. I'm thinking of doing a course at college, and I'm considering being a volunteer at the library. Yes, overall life's not all bad, although I still suffer from depression.

Sharon

My home was really important to me. Like Sharon, I felt it necessary to sell my house. Too many memories and too big now in any case. I did not find it easy leaving behind the home that had been a place of much joy, as well as great sadness. And it took another move beyond that before I found the privacy and security I desired. I wanted to stay close to family and friends, to have access to things that mattered, and to have a garden where I could enjoy nature with Peter's little dog. Here, I could replenish my depleted emotional and physical resources. Things I would once have considered indulgent, like spending an entire day reading or pottering in the garden, were enriching.

The trees breathed life into me. The sun gave me energy. The birds, insects, and animals shared their world as one. We breathed the same air. I was part of nature. Just as sorrow had stolen my immunity, this living magic was returning it to me.

I could toil. I could rest. I was connected with the soil, the warm earth. I observed a fragile frond pushing through to the daylight, seemingly against all odds, unfolding, turning its face to the sun, opening its leaves and letting them grow to absorb more energy. I could do the same. If a soft bud could swell with Life, so could I.

It was restorative, this affair with the healing powers of nature. This need for tranquility, for contemplation was fundamental. What pain had poisoned, nature could cure. My own body was the instrument of healing. I began to respect it. Peter's dog became my dog. She loved walking on the headland. So did I. There was something in the sea air. Moments of melancholy tried clinging, tenaciously, but the strong ocean breeze dried my tears.

At last, I began to feel.

Others told me about emerging from their blanket of grief as well:

*After Scott's suicide I was in a really bad way. My sister came and stayed with me until the funeral was over. She did everything for me. I just couldn't do anything. But her family needed her too, so she went back home. I ended up living with them a few years later when I was sick.*

*It wasn't planned that I would move in with them, it just happened. I needed Jane's support so much, and she didn't ask questions, the way that someone close doesn't need to. Her family just accepted that I was there, and I didn't feel like a stranger. It was comforting to have them around me, you know just living life. The kids were in and out with so many different things in their lives, and my brother-in-law is quiet but helped with lots of practical things. He helped me work out my finances as well and then, when I was ready, he helped me use Scott's insurance payout to buy my apartment. My family was there for me when I needed them, and now I can manage on my own, but I still see them every week.*

*Now that I live on my own, I have time to do things I've often thought of doing but never got around to. I love dancing and go to salsa every week. I love it. I have taken up patchwork and met some really lovely people. I have also joined an orchid club. I don't have much space, but they don't need much, and they are so lovely.*

Tammy

No longer constantly in my mind. No longer constantly feeling sick. I had stumbled and at times felt absolutely defeated by the effort required to emerge into my converted life. I had to face the past before I could let it go. I had to traipse through memories of my own, from before I had met Peter, to understand myself. I had to get to know that person again to understand where resilience had resided. It was that person, naïve and inexperienced, who steadied the turmoil of grief. Grateful for that inner reserve, somehow I began to accept suicide as part of life. As part of my life.

# Chapter 11

# Acceptance

Suicide, that sad and lonely death, is a stark demonstration of the intimate connection binding the mind, body, and spirit. If one aspect of life is out-of-kilter, it affects another. Peter's secret and dreadful pain of his soul, his psychache, had prompted him to remove the body in which his distress dwelt. It could not sit isolated, removed from his whole being. It's host, its other part—his body—had died to remove it.

Beyond his deeply personal experience, his unendurable burden, was his intricate connection with other people. Had there been no link, no love, no bond, I would feel no grief. Distraught by Death. Obsessed by the agonizing conundrum of self-death.

***AD—Year 5.*** *As I let him go, slowly, slowly, I feel an emptiness, a place where he lived, now barely a shadow, more a scar. It chokes me still but releases as I turn to face a new day, a new life. I must or I, too, will be lost.*

*Is it possible to feel contentment again, to be released from this agony, to know that life goes on, to feel it, to be part of it?*

*It has taken time, more time than I expected, but the weight is lifting. I do not need to carry this load like the albatross. It will always be part of who I am, but the obsession, the noose of doom, the acceptance of responsibility, is diminishing.*

*I bring this new feeling, this new identity, into my core as I walk along the beach, the wind, the sea, the wild beauty filling my soul. The soul that I thought was empty. The soul that I thought could never be filled again. I feel the sweetness of life. The sweetness of this vastness. The sweetness of this earth. The sweetness of the infinite skies.*

*I do not forget—cannot forget—but the intense focus on his death finds a place alongside the rest of life, and of death, of the inevitable binding of the two, of the timelessness of nature. The cycle of life. Its transience. Its impermanence. Death belongs to us all.*

I feel this grief in the core of my being. I had felt isolated with my sadness, yet the fact that I grieved signified the kindred spirit that joins us all, the invisible thread that unites each of us with other human beings. We exist within relationships, within families, within groups of friends, within communities, within a social structure where we interact with, and rely upon, others for a sense of belonging.

My most intimate and important relationship had been broken, leaving me hurt, confused, and lost. By staring into my grief, acknowledging it, and allowing myself to become reconciled with Death and the cause of death, I felt I could become more than a survivor of suicide. As I incorporated Peter's loss as part of who I am, it ceased to dominate me.

By not allowing the suicide to define me, I began to emerge from my grief as a changed person, able to embrace a new and satisfying life. I connected with those I knew in a fresh way. I found new friendships. I did new things. I needed to avoid the abyss of sadness. I learned to live again. To do this, I needed time, security, and love. It took a startlingly long time before I ceased to be consumed by Peter's death.

The time frame, and the process, are different for all of us. Mine was not a linear process, and at times, my deep sorrow took me unaware. I had heard various ideas about when grief is "supposed to" finish, but it is a never-ending process. Yet there is room for some kind of acceptance, even for resolution. Suicide grief may never be put to rest fully, but it seemed that I was beginning to be released from its intensity. Gina described this delicate change:

*People kept telling me that time would heal, and that sickening feeling does get less. But I'm not sure that heal is the right word. I feel it is more that I'm used to it now. Everything is different, and there is a lot you just plain can't get used to, but there is also this instinct, that life goes on, and I want to be part of it. I want to keep living, not be pushed down by this huge weight of sorrow.*

*I think I knew this at the beginning, but the bleakness wouldn't let me go. Maybe I was living on adrenaline then as well. I can't honestly say that I remember that much about the first year, or even two. It is a blur, and I think I was a little crazy quite frankly. Time gives you the ability to let all the pieces fall somewhere, although some of it is pretty weird. I certainly feel different, completely changed, emptier, and numb in many ways, but stronger. I am not ecstatically happy, but then I'm not sad all the time either.*

*My emphasis is different. I get a lot of satisfaction from my work. I work in HR, so people are a big part of my job. I like that. And I go out a lot. But on my own. I am beginning to like my independence, although I don't want to end up on my own. I have no idea if I will ever have another close relationship. For the moment, I am content just to be.*

Gina

I needed emotional and physical security. Like Sharon, Tammy, and me, others needed to move from their domestic situations, especially if the suicide had occurred there. Some chose to stay. Some had no choice. I found the process of letting go in this way helpful, at least symbolically.

As I removed personal items, it seemed to figuratively free Peter's spirit. It wasn't formal, but I did have rituals of lighting candles and playing special music that seemed to smooth the process. For a long time, I had carefully chosen special mementoes around as *aides-mémoires*. But gradually these lost prominence.

Joanne had a special area for remembrance:

*My family has a tradition where our grandparents' photos were displayed in a special place after they died, or anyone else. I had a cousin who died when she was young. My parents had photos of her and of their parents on top of a sideboard. I didn't really absorb the significance of it when I was younger, but my mum would light a candle if it was their birthday or another special time, like Easter or Christmas. I just sort of knew that's what you do, so I did that for Sally. It just feels right. I found it so painful when I first did it, and I put her photo away, as I couldn't bear to look at it, but a while ago, I took it out again, and now I leave it out. It's in the hallway, and I pass it every day and just say, "hello."*

Joanne

As I began to reintegrate with my family and friends, I found strength in their love. A different love from the one I had lost but, nevertheless, a wonderful connection with the living rather than the dead. I became buoyed by this love, and it helped carry me from the darkness into the light. Love has the potential to dissipate shadows.

I have gained a penetrating awareness of the transitory nature of life. The knowledge that one day we all will die, that nothing remains the same. I had not appreciated this concept to the degree I was now experiencing it. Our world is changeable, mutable, and dynamic. Inconstancy is constant. Everything alters. Our existence is deeply connected to the immediate environment, the world, and the universe beyond. We all respond to the perpetual movement of the earth, sun, and moon. Seasons come and go, life comes and goes.

I came to accept a life gone as part of our ever-changing world. I could regret this loss, feel sad, and resist accepting my altered situation, but eventually, I had to incorporate these changes into my daily life. They became familiar. It was not easy, and I didn't want them, but these changes became part of who I am.

Over a period of time, I became more finely tuned to messages I believe Peter had tried to give me, and this altered my interpretation of our relationship. What had appeared to be indifference, I began to see was probably disassociation, part of his transition toward relieving his pain. My response of hurt and anger diminished, and I felt more empathetic to the anguish he must have felt. Tracey's experiences also gave her more compassion for her partner:

*I began to have more understanding of how Joe felt, especially after I went through that low, dark period of depression myself. I can't say that I will ever understand it totally, such a terrible death, and trying to work out how it must have felt for him, but I do feel more at peace about it now. I can't explain it, but it is sort of like, well that's part of life, dying I mean.*

Tracey

The impact felt like the repercussions of the movement of a tectonic plate or the eruption of a submerged volcano—an unseen shift that destabilizes the ocean floor. Displaced water has to go somewhere. The closer it comes to land, the more pressure builds up until, finally, a tsunami forms. Being swept up by this tsunami was devastating. I felt as if I could never find footing on dry land. Gasping for air and searching for any means of survival, it was hard to resist the forcefulness as it threatened to destroy me.

Yet I had ridden through the immensity of the tsunami, taking sanctuary on the ocean floor of my core being, allowing the mighty wave to wash over me. I was able to evade the worst ravages of this catastrophe. I had learned to yield to that which I could not control and trust that the cyclic nature of life would protect me.

# Chapter 12

## Resolution

My feelings were constantly altering. As each insight, each subtle change, occurred, I adjusted to its impact. At times acute, at others less persistent, I became acquainted with sorrow and its blinding pain, and I allowed it shape.

I had been stunned by the suggestion that it takes years for grief to subside. Daunted and overwhelmed, I couldn't imagine that the misery I was experiencing could be endured for so long. Seven years, I heard. The biblical seven years. Unimaginable. An eternity. How could the agony of grieving be sustained? Was it not obvious that the burden of grief, the horror, and the pain could not be tolerated for such an extensive period? Seven seconds, seven minutes, seven hours, long enough, but seven years!

And yet, seven years passed, as predicted, sometimes mellow, sometimes potent, but they passed nevertheless. Getting older. It happens to us all. Time! Everyone says that time is the healer. Is it? How can time heal? How much time? I was stuck on seven. It seems that even our bodies are tuned into sevens. Our cells replace themselves over various lengths of time. Once I read that it takes seven years for this to occur throughout our entire body, implying that physically, we are not the same person we were seven years ago. This surely is simplistic. There is no unified change; we don't shed our skins as snakes. Hard science or not, the appeal is symbolic! Prophetic time!

"Sitting shiva," the period of mourning for those of the Jewish faith, is seven days. Literal or figurative, the concept of cycles of seven is a repeated theme throughout human life. It even embraces music and color. Without any base other than supposition, I hung onto this idea, that after seven years I would feel different. I longed for the anxiety to leave, to feel joy, to feel light and free.

I focused on the epiphany and missed the subtlety. It arrived, not in a flurry but as the gradual and incremental lessening of the intense fear of living, of the timid trying-on of an emerging persona. Not suddenly, not dramatically, the load began to shift. I could breathe slowly and deeply again. It took me a while to realize that I had slid into, and taken ownership of, many changes within myself.

*AD—Year 7. Stillness does not come easily. I resist. I feel changed. Despite my resistance, I am absorbing Peter's loss into my life. His death sits within me. It is not separate, nor has it vanished. Just as in life, Peter is part of who I am. The loneliness has lessened. I feel less awkward on* my own. I no longer seek an audience for my innermost thoughts. I am less obsessed by Peter's sudden, immutable departure. It cannot be changed. It just is.

Equally, there are things I cannot accept graciously. I still stumble at how it happened. Although I no longer feel nauseated at the thought of that violent and brutal death, and the acute despair has dispersed, the sadness lies close. My head has told me many things, but there remains a deep disbelief that Peter could have done this. Lack of resolution, denial, complicated grief. I may answer to these, but still I love life, hurting or not, I appreciate this precious gift. Happiness and sadness living side-by-side. It is, after all, the human condition to embrace both sides of the same coin. Good and bad, black and white, yin and yang. Can they mutate? Are they one and the same? Is gray the real color? I don't believe so. Our world is alive with color. All the colors of the rainbow. The rainbow, traditionally thought to join life with death, has many perspectives—as I found once on a plane trip, seen from above, rainbows are round, a full circle. A rainbow circle. This is life! To me this is life—full of color and continuous. Never-ending, like the symbol for infinity.

Just as it was impossible for me to measure the quantity of my grief, its quality escaped measurement as well. Its mercurial nature was attached to the past, the present, and the future. My perception of Peter, our relationship, and the way he had chosen to die churned in my innermost being. It took me a long time to shift my dreadful angst from horror and self-blame to the greater understanding and empathy I have now for suicidal torment.

I was curious to see how the others were faring. I had overlapped with a few who had shared their stories, but several had touched my life only briefly. Mia and I met again. She spoke more freely, with far less anxiety. We discussed how she was feeling now, several years after her husband, Alex, had hanged himself:

I needed to be by myself. I still do, but less so. I like coming home to my little flat, closing the door, ignoring the phone, and just being with my immense feelings. Well, I guess it has actually become a habit. I have my privacy, and I really love it.

I'm in a completely different space from where I was before. I live in my own flat, just enough for me. It is more than living on my own. It shows I have a new life now.

Overall, I'm actually quite happy. My flat is convenient. I can walk to the train and the shops. I have many interests and friends. I traveled overseas for the first time last year and loved it. I went with a friend, but I'm thinking of going on my own next time.

My son and his wife had a little boy, and it has helped bring us back together. New life is very healing. I visit them in their new home, and sometimes I look after my grandson. He gives me great happiness.

I don't think of the suicide much anymore. It was sad. Well really, really dreadful, actually. I don't like to remember that part. So I just get on with my own life. I see my sister, and I have new friends through my new interests.

I am not interested in getting close to anyone, though. I don't want a new relationship. I don't trust anyone anymore. My life is different, but I'm getting used to it.

Mia

I made contact with Carole, and we met up again about four years after she first told me her story. She looked and seemed quite different. Although there was still sorrow in her eyes, she smiled more and appeared calmer and quieter:

I had been so down. I really thought I would never feel happy again. I felt rejected. Twice. First by the secrecy of our relationship, and then by his suicide. Not being able to grieve openly really got to me. I began to realize that I was getting worse and worse. I didn't see anyone, didn't talk to anyone, got touchy at work. They all seemed to forget about Marty at work. Talked about it for a bit, then he just seemed to fade away. I was beside myself with grief but didn't know how to express it. I was frightened of letting the cat out of the bag, so to speak, and at the same time wanting to tell everyone. You would think that would have been to protect his wife, or Marty's memory, but it really was because I didn't want them blaming me.

I ended up going to a counselor, well two actually, as the first wasn't much use. But the one I still see encouraged me to acknowledge my relationship and acknowledge Marty's suicide. As I faced that, I could see that I was really trapped and very negative. It took me a while to gain the courage to do it, but eventually, I found a new job. When I left that old firm, where I'd been with Marty, it was like getting a new lease on life. I've been in my new job over two years now, and, boy, it feels good. And believe this or not, I met someone on one of those dating sites on the Internet, and we see each other regularly. He has been through stuff too, so we have been able to support each other. I think it will work out. So am I in a different place? You bet!

Carole

I was encouraged by meeting up again with Mia and Carole and decided to follow up some of the others. I found Evan, slimmer and definitely happier:

Since I saw you last, it must be some time now. I've changed. Eventually I got up off the couch and stopped wasting my gym fees. It was the health scare that did it for me. One day, I just said to myself, "get a grip," and I've improved ever since. I've lost the weight I put on and have a great partner. We're thinking of getting married.

I walk every day. Marie, my new partner, often comes with me. It is like a tonic. I was heading toward high blood pressure and high blood sugar, but since I've been walking, that's improved. It's just that I feel better. Occasionally I freak out, and I really don't like it when Marie takes a bath. She understands though, as I've told her all about it. And there are little things that trigger memories, and I feel sick, but I can control it more now. I have to tell myself that it's over, that horrible moment of finding her cold and so wet. It still chokes me up. I have to put it behind me, or I will drown too.

Evan

What I was finding was that time did change feelings and attitudes. It didn't remove the pain, but it allowed the opportunity to process it and incorporate it into the ever-changing kaleidoscope of life:

*Well, I'm not the same, that's for sure. More, sort of, quiet, and I think about things a lot more. You know, like in perspective. I don't worry so much about little things; they don't matter. It shows you what's important. For me, it's family and some friends. Nothing else matters.*

Carrie

Change didn't come easily. Life went on around all of us. I certainly felt different, not only from who I had been before Peter's death but also, who I became afterward kept changing. A perpetual readjustment. Sometimes I was surprised by my response. I was living in a world that simultaneously was sorrowful and soothing. A previously unfamiliar depth crept in. I felt excluded from what appeared to me to be frivolous. I could not reach that lightness, but I did have a muted sense of enjoyment. I felt this same sense of reserve when I spoke to Sharon:

*My entire life has turned around, from happiness to nightmare to more, well, a bit removed from it all, really. I was really struggling when I saw you before. I was in such a deep hole for a long, long time. Everything seemed to pile in on top of me. My kids were depressed, and I just couldn't do anything to help. My Mum was unwell. I looked after her for about nine months, and in some ways, it was good to have a purpose, but when she died, it threw me right into the depths of despair again. Like everyone I loved seemed to be dead. Of course, I love my kids and they're not dead. They are both much more settled now and have moved on with their lives. I have too. I mean I actually have. It took me a while to relax into my new home, but I think I'll be all right.*

Sharon

Rowena, too, found her life radically changed:

The last few years have been unbelievably painful and difficult. In some ways, I got lost in caring for the kids and going to work. So many times I woke panicking in the night. The bills kept accumulating. I was working full-time and trying to cope with everything. You know—fixing things in the house, the car, the kids, their school, school holidays—pressure, pressure, pressure. I nearly cracked lots of times. I got so angry with Mick. Felt it was all his fault. Well, it was, but of course it wasn't. He couldn't help it. I know that now. I know he was sick. I have come to understand that more. My friend's cousin hanged himself a while ago now, and we have talked about it a lot. I didn't talk to anyone for ages, and the anger and horror just grew inside of me. I got really sick. I had sick leave luckily but not much. I used to dream of some place I could go and just be looked after. Somewhere I didn't have to think or be responsible for everything.

I think it was having my friend to talk to that started to help me. I got close to my aunt as well. I never had been before, but I had to ask her to look after the kids once, and she just became part of our lives. She found out about a support group and came with me. It was very emotional. Someone told me about a counselor who I could see six times for free. I went for that, but I haven't been back. I can't afford it. But it helped break the ice—into thinking and talking and being more accepting.

And of course, the kids are older now, so it's easier. I worry about them—if they'll have their father's troubles. It took a lot out of them, and I feel guilty, but they know I love them, and they are nice kids really. Then there was a neighbor of my aunt's who I met when he came round to help my aunt. He was separated from his partner and little girl, and he started to join in our family life. I think we all filled a space for him. He is so gentle, and hurt, but he has helped me deal with the pain. Recently we started a relationship—like two wounded animals—but he's the best thing that happened to me, apart from my kids. I even laugh now—and feel happy sometimes. I wonder if he will leave me too. He has made a big difference to my life, just being there for me, so I need to learn to trust him.

My girlfriend helped me understand that Mick was sick—and the support group. There were so many other people suffering from suicide. I didn't realize it was so common. I do feel like there's a future now. Not just working and feeling sad and angry all the time.

Rowena

Finding out how others were managing was reassuring. I seemed to be absorbing my anxieties. Time was playing its part. It gave a place for grief to rest, a place where I could view resolution as a possibility.

I needed space where judgment was removed, where I could redefine my expectations and acknowledge my transforming life. My perceptions were constantly being revised and updated. I realized that I could not live in the past; I had to live in the present. Life went on. I wanted to be part of it. Dreadful as my experiences had been, a strong sense that life was for living, not something to be endured, drove me forward.

Time unaided did not obliterate my deep sorrow. It did not move forward becoming incrementally positive. Beyond linear, chronological time was *Kairos*, "the fullness of time," the significance of what time means. I could remember certain events and feelings but couldn't always remember the exact day, month, or year these happened. Yet these meaningful memories punctuated my life. They were fluid, mirroring my feelings and intersecting with sequential, precise, and measured time. Time has quality as well as quantity.

Time was where Peter's illness had incubated. And it was where I hoped to find solace. As I counted the days, nights, weeks, and years from Peter's death moments of panic, happiness, sadness, joy, and anger all existed without order. This jumble required a calmness before I could locate resilience.

Time provided familiarity. It helped me become accustomed to my pain, but without acknowledging and ultimately freeing my anxieties, my wound would remain unhealed. Left alone, my grief could fester, and, like any other infection, erupt unexpectedly or spread throughout my body and make me sick. Yet I not only had hung onto chronological time as being the ultimate healer, I also prescribed the length of time that this should take. Time for grieving cannot be defined. It was working through the pain and letting it go that helped me, not how long it took. Nevertheless, for me, and for some of the others, this took time. Gradually, grief relinquished its prime position and became incorporated into my whole being. Never coming to rest completely, however.

Facing Peter's death, acknowledging it, and accepting it lessened my pain. When I resisted, my pain was heightened. If I tensed against my fear, a protective shield formed around me, as if alerting me to danger and increasing my anxiety. Hindering me from feeling life again. The barrier had to be removed. Chronological time was significant, but it was not a solo solution.

# Chapter 13

## Release

I recalled a story Peter had told me some time ago that had given me an insight into how unnecessary baggage can weigh someone down. Peter was an adventurer. He loved the thrill of outdoor life. Many years ago, he was scuba diving with some friends in a beautiful harbor. A tropical paradise. It was a magnificent opportunity to feel at one with nature. Peter and his companions piled into their boat, and, full of the enthusiasm of youth, they were motoring across the bay. The sun was shining, with a soft wind whipping the waves and adding to their excitement. The wooden-hulled boat rose and fell, slapping against the water.

Without warning, the boat came down on something hard, probably a log. In an instant, the seemingly solid hull had a gaping hole. Salt water quickly filled the boat. There was a scramble as the young men all grabbed anything they could. Most of their belongings sank rapidly.

Peter was able to secure his air tank, mask, and snorkel, hurriedly putting them on as the boat disappeared from under him. Land was in sight, and they signaled to each other to make for shore. They were all young and fit, and no one was injured. With the bonus of his diving equipment, Peter decided to swim underwater instead of battling the choppy surface with waves continually washing over his face.

As he headed off, he could see his companions above. They began to pull away from him. He swam faster to keep up. Faster and harder. But he could not keep up. He wondered why. He was a strong swimmer, he could breathe, but still, his companions moved farther away.

He wondered what it was that was slowing him down. There was something in his hand. A rope. Attached to the rope was a plastic bucket. That would be handy to bail out the boat as it filled with water. He swam harder, trying to maintain momentum so the bucket would not sink. But it was dragging him down.

Then he realized he didn't need the bucket. It was of no use now. The reason for having the bucket had gone, and now it was filled with seawater that he didn't need either. The effort of dragging the superfluous bucket through the water was pulling him farther into the depths and risking his life. What could he do?

He let it go.

In letting it go, he saved himself. Years later, he may have symbolically returned to pick up that bucket and allow it to drag him to the bottom of the ocean.

As I remembered his story, I could see that I was carrying around a load I didn't need either. It was weighing me down and dragging me under until I was emotionally exhausted.

I was drowning in my own despair. The solution was simple. I needed to let it go.

I had to learn this skill. Consciously. It was up to me to acknowledge my sadness and incorporate it into my life. Slowly and deliberately severing each ethereal cord that had drawn me tight into the darkness.

My life was beginning to change. I was becoming less consumed by my own needs.

One of my sons shared his feelings:

*As Peter's son, I would like to offer my perspective on suicide, in the hope that it might provide a light at the end of a dark and lonely tunnel. Many of the experiences and emotions written about in this book are familiar to me. After my father's death, I spent more time than I can consciously recall in what seemed like an inescapable vortex of negative thoughts and emotions, inside of which time was being sucked up so quickly that I was unable to deal with daily life. Problems were blown out of proportion, and I saw paranoid meaning in actions, words, and situations that were in fact innocuous. It was impossible for others to do anything constructive to help me, and I felt helpless to help myself. Now I feel differently.*

*Turning the tide on a tsunami of grief following the suicide of a loved one is no easy feat, let's be honest. It's not something that happens overnight. It is a long and slow process that we move toward step by step, acknowledging that setbacks are inevitable but maintaining the desire to find a way forward. At least that's how it has been for me.*

*But there are a few things worth knowing if you do wish to find your way out of the turmoil. Oddly enough, I owe much of this knowledge* to my late father, who was a great teacher and usually an inspiring role model of morality and strength. The point was made earlier in the book by my mother, that even in his final moments, he showed great commitment and strength to what he probably perceived as his duty. It might seem perverse, but I think that people who take their own lives usually feel it is the right thing for them to be doing.

Each one of us has a different story to tell; we each experience life differently and have different beliefs that influence the way we rationalize and internalize the events of our lives, and from my perspective, it is those beliefs that hold the key to surviving the "suicide tsunami."

My father taught me many things, but his most profound wisdom is this: The events in our lives can have radically different impacts and significance, depending upon our perspective of those events and our willingness to move beyond them. For some people, any event is a chance to find dissatisfaction, while for others, it seems that they bounce back happily and effortlessly from one situation to the next. The "trick" to this has, I believe, more to do with attitude and willingness than with luck or biology. What this means to me is that the key to finding a way out is to focus more on positive emotions than on negative ones; this does not mean that we can deny our negative emotions—they are always there—but we do not allow them full control over our lives. A useful metaphor might be that we relegate our negative emotions to the role of passenger rather than driver.

I have experienced many, or perhaps most or even all of the crippling, negative emotions that other readers have experienced, but they no longer reflect how things are for me. The past is not something that we have control over, but it is possible to design a better future for ourselves. This begins by recognizing that there is little value in allowing negative emotions to control us. In practice, this is, of course, a terribly difficult thing for most people, but as previously mentioned, the key to making this a reality is to accept and stay focused on the fact that you wish to change. For me, I remain focused on the idea that happiness is the place where I want to arrive and where I want to stay. If you take one moment at a time, this can become your reality as it is becoming mine. I have moments of negativity, but this is no longer my predominant perspective.

I believe that there is a scale of perspectives, or perceptions, that begin in the negative arena and, slowly, rise in positivity. The bottom of this scale might be "hate all things and circumstances," while the top of the scale might be "selfless love for all things and circumstances." We can all experience the full range of these perceptions, but the longer we dwell on one, the harder it becomes to experience the others. What this means is that we are all primarily looking at life through one of the perceptions on this scale. I think that the border between negative and positive emotions lies at the point of having the courage to make a change.

Once you decide to look for happiness, it begins to unfold in front of you.

People who seem to be doomed to negativity tend to stay focused on the lower levels of awareness, while those who manage to move forward are able to rise out of the negative arena into the positive arena. If we are aware of this and strive at all times, in all situations, to move our own state of awareness up to at least the next level, then we are on the right path. I am not suggesting that we should ignore or forget our grief but that we should relegate it to the second or third or fourth shelf down! Why do we need to keep it in the forefront of our minds? Some people will feel guilt or other negative emotions if they replace their grief with more positive emotion, but what magical value does grief have that means we have to hang onto it? None! Let it go! From my perspective, holding onto grief defines the life of our loved one by his or her final act and neglects the fullness of the life that came before. We are also halting our own life and the lives of those around us. There is nothing to be gained, nor is there any honor in acting this way; it is ultimately selfish and should be transcended. Guilt is natural, but we must strive to move beyond it, to make it a less powerful part of ourselves. We should honor ourselves, those we've lost, and, perhaps most importantly of all, those who are still around by finding the courage to move forward with positivity.

*Maintaining a positive attitude comes from a deep calmness that is inside each of us.*

It is not the realm of a few; it's part of us all, and we have the ability to find it. I am fortunate enough to have people around who allow me personal space to grieve or simply be grumpy when I need it. Not everybody has this luxury, but it is the selflessness of others that allows me to transcend my selfishness. If you do not have people in your life who can offer this kind of support then I would suggest seeking them out. My family are my guardian angels. We can all find supportive people, but we must learn to see them, and this takes courage. Having a support team means that we are free to search deep within ourselves to find that knowledge I spoke of previously. There is a calm place inside us all that is capable of supplying an endless amount of strength, compassion, love, and positivity. To find it is possible, although it requires focus and dedication.

Although I can identify with many of the feelings expressed by others who have been through the suicide of a loved one, I no longer find that these negative feelings dominate me. In fact, I no longer have anything more than the occasional feeling of sadness that my kids do not have their grandfather to play with or answer their questions. During his life, he was an inspiration to many; he touched numerous people around the world with his wit and compassion. He was a very rare person who is missed by all who knew him. The emotion that I experience in relation to his death is now more a sense of responsibility that I have to keep his legacy alive, and although his death was an untimely loss, I am thankful for the time we spent together and for the growth that he allowed me to experience in both his life and death.

Rob

# Chapter 14

# Reflections

Peter's final solution lives with me. The consequences of suicide don't begin and end within a defined timeframe. Nor do they follow a prescribed pattern. Grief does not go away. It continues. It was learning to acknowledge, accept, and incorporate change that freed me from my intense and consuming sadness. Although my life is different now, it is nevertheless fulfilling and rewarding. And while there are times when I feel betrayed by my own naiveté, there equally are others when I'm more accommodating of what I cannot change. My life has altered dramatically, and even though it has not turned out as I imagined, it is still satisfying. Although I live with many reminders of Peter's fateful decision, had I not indulged my compulsive curiosity, I would never have been able to find peace. Not everyone feels this way. For many it is far too painful and perhaps seems futile.

Insight into Peter's excruciating and recurring emotional pain has helped me come to terms with his death. As he struggled with his abject despair, he must have been distraught, trying to find answers when it's likely he didn't fully understand the problem himself. I will always feel compassion for his pain, but now it is the living who hurt.

One of the most difficult aspects I found was feeling that no one else could comprehend my horror or sense of betrayal and abandonment. Perhaps that is why hearing the experiences of others was so reassuring. I spoke with many more people than appear in this book and have not ceased to be amazed how suicide sits silently as a private pain. Yet despite my initial feelings of being alone in my pain, there is compassion for the bereaved, and help available. I even found there are many people who have no direct association with suicide who care deeply and are willing to assist, even at the darkest of times. I will forever be grateful to those who joined me along the way, who unstintingly supported my vacillating emotions without judgment. I also am indebted to the friends and strangers who bravely opened up to me. Their generosity made my life more bearable, and, I hope, it also made a positive difference to theirs.

I found all the stories I heard, and continue to hear, deeply moving, and hearing them gives me a perverted sense of comfort through a sense of belonging. Most who appear here are now removed from their acute pain, although all agree that suicide has had a huge impact upon their lives. Even though the experiences of the people who shared their stories varied, there were many commonalities as well. It seems to me that at the heart of these were difficulty in understanding and accepting suicide; guilt at not being able to prevent the suicide; feeling that suicide is shameful; and feeling rejected by the person who suicided. These themes were repeated. A number of people commented that feeling that suicide was a choice made it hard to accept.

I am aware that others have fresh wounds. I hope that reading our combined experiences provides some kind of reassurance that the pain can lessen and life can again be meaningful. Increased information certainly released me from constantly defining my life through Peter's death. By doing this, I was not only erasing how he lived, it was destructive and dangerous for me as well. Having empathy for the unrelenting agony that forced Peter's hand and acknowledging his death as part of life have freed me. Seeking answers and trying to understand allowed me to accept our tragic story. It gave me the opportunity to absorb this into who I am, allowing it to shape rather than dominate me.

Without doubt, I have changed. However, good counseling helped me reframe my perspective, and I was able to ease my existential angst through delving into philosophical and spiritual teachings. Empathy for Peter, acknowledging my own pain, and redirecting my focus to the living from the dead has released my oppressive despair. Thus I have been able to embrace a subdued kind of contentment where I do not have to serve a life sentence of crippling sorrow.

One positive outcome is that I have come to appreciate my own strengths and those of my children that previously I had not acknowledged. I realized that each of us was called upon many times to go beyond the realms of everyday experience. In hindsight, I see, these difficulties gave us confidence and courage. Thus the ramifications of suicide, and living with someone who is depressive, are multifaceted.

There should be no blame or shame related to suicide. Usually there are both, in great measure. Suicide sparks polarized opinions. Some people believe that it is exercising an individual right, the right to choose when and how to die. I falter with this concept. To me, it makes the assumption that we are disconnected from one another. If this were true, Peter's death would barely have had any impact upon our children, family, friends, and me. Neither would others suffer from their losses. Philosophically, the debate overlaps euthanasia, a contentious concept. While humane "putting down" of animals seems to be almost universally accepted, deliberate human death is another matter. Loaded with subjectivity, religious overtones, and legal complexities, there are fine and mobile lines when it comes to intentional human death.

Although I would not have wished Peter's torment to continue, his unilateral decision disempowered me, or anyone else, from helping to ease his burden. I believe that there are less radical ways of treating psychache than solitary obliteration. Rights are counterbalanced by responsibility. Accepting that our actions have consequences can influence our decisions. Ironically, it could be argued that some suicidal people are motivated by this sense, believing that their deaths will help others. So what could appear to be a selfish act might, in fact, be intended as selfless; misjudging the impact of shock, sorrow, and social pressures that can destabilize families and communities.

Until suicide sits in the open as a social issue, silence will remain the enemy. While groups like doctors, paramedics, police, and the military continue to bear the public burdens of trauma and violence without appropriate support; while the mentally ill do not have access to unprejudiced and good quality treatment; while we make little allowance for emotional sensitivity, we will continue to lose community members to suicide. Perhaps we are now reaping the rewards of a world that is fast and shallow, obsessed with economic outcomes and narcissistic individualism. Suicide may be the symptom alerting us that all is not well.

As I move away from my tragedy, suicide is still a daily event. Nothing has held back the tidal wave. Suicide remains a major avoidable death. Exposing it, encouraging dialogue, and removing judgment erode its power. There are now many organizations dedicated to increasing awareness of suicide. Education, wide discussion, and readily available preventive strategies seem a more positive direction to head than accepting suicide as a given individual right or labeling it as the end result of a mental disorder. Public awareness of the terrible impact of suicide helps break the isolation of silence.

For all of this understanding, my own battle with anxiety was not over. Just as some kind of equilibrium seemed within my grasp, other life events triggered those familiar feelings of nausea, trembling, and racing heart as a tight band of apprehension gripped my stomach. My veneer of passivity lifted, and fear griped my cool rationality. An uncontrolled beast stirred within. Panic! So memorable. I knew that sick despair well. I had practiced it when it didn't deserve such prominence. Again, I felt I was drowning in a persistent ocean of emotional distress.

I had learned in times of uncertainty to assume disaster. If one of my children didn't answer the phone, I would imagine they had suicided. If the dog wasn't in the kitchen, I thought she had been run over. Bypassing reason. Go directly to jail. I wanted my family around where I could see them. No amount of rational argument had removed dread as my initial response to their absence.

Overly sensitive feelings lay close to the surface. I sought counseling—years later. It helped. The expert counseling I received helped me to become familiar with what had happened. I learned to recognize my anxiety. I began to look more easily at my panic responses without the barrier of terror closing around me, blocking my senses to that which I could not accept. By avoiding anything that compromised my emotions, I felt I was protecting myself from further hurt, but I was forcing away good feelings as well. I learned to observe myself, Peter, and our lives together. As my memories unfolded, they lost their potency. I learned to witness through new understandings, to accommodate and accept that which I could not change. Blame gave way to tolerance. Guilt to reflection. And fear to reassurance.

I have heard words that are intended to comfort suggesting that the worst thing that could happen has happened. Yet other people die unexpectedly. Other people suicide. Acknowledging this is not necessarily a fanciful overreaction. Sometimes suicides cluster. There have been two in my family. Losing someone to suicide is not the worst thing that can happen. Tragedies can multiply. What makes a difference is how we relate to what happens.

I feel that my intricate relationship with Peter reinforces the significance of the connection we all have with other people. We are simultaneously individual and interconnected. I was not only mourning the loss of my primary relationship, I was also suffering from subsequent losses and changes in other relationships. I could sink into this vortex or strive for a way out. I couldn't do it unaided. I needed bonds with other people to help release me from my pain. Joining others along the way brought a richness I couldn't find alone. My family, friends, and colleagues supported me as I constantly recreated myself. They became the threads that wove through my life, constructing the tapestry that is stronger than a single thread. Gradually I re-engaged with the world around me.

I have no magical answers, just the will to live the best I can. Initially, I had been emotionally paralyzed by fear, shut off to the world around me. I overworked myself so there was no time or energy to nurture my grieving soul. As I began to accept that suicide was no one's fault, I was able to forgive and let go. This made way for trust, intuition, and spirituality to resurface.

Tangible changes seemed necessary for me. Moving house, selling Peter's business, resuming my maiden name, nurturing my health, finding a new work environment, and eventually retiring all assisted my acceptance of the alterations Peter's death made to my life. These are visible statements of my emotional metamorphosis.

Beyond the rational, I engage with spiritual dimensions of life and have found a tranquility that escaped me in my pursuit of practical answers. The best advice I can offer is to listen to your soul, give it voice, then accept it as fundamental to your whole being. In doing this, I have been able to move away from my fixation with gloom. By allowing my ego to dominate, my anxiety and the need to control everything around me took over. Trusting my inner voice, sitting quietly underneath the raging tempest of fear and guilt, and recognizing the innate calmness of my core being helped me.

I learned that I had choices. Although initially I had found it too difficult to face my grief, I was able to let it in incrementally, examine it, own it, and let it live within me. Not as a destructive force but resting gently. I could either allow it to consume me or acknowledge and accept it.

It seemed the ultimate healing came with forgiveness, letting go what had hurt me. I had to embrace this release as a freedom that allows me to live with integrity. I have not found accepting loss easy. Accepting loss through suicide seems particularly painful. As I was preparing this book, unhappy memories resurfaced. Memories that, in part, I would rather have left undisturbed. However, bringing them out, examining them, and acknowledging their existence has allowed me to integrate them into my entire being as only an aspect of who I am. Sadness and regret have a part, not the entire stage. I have been able to release the forceful distress of disbelief, of questioning and constant sorrow. I have stepped away from the tempest to embrace a calmer place. Thus, for me, writing has been cathartic. Peter's suicide no longer eclipses my life.

In losing Peter, I looked into the depths of what makes us human. I saw it, felt it, tossed it about, wore it, and emerged with a more reflective understanding. I learned that I couldn't change that fateful moment. I could only shape my reaction to it. I learned that if I define myself by only one facet of who I am, to the exclusion of others, I lose my sense of balance. I learned that life is a fragile and precious gift lent to us for safekeeping. I learned that I could ease the suffering created by suicide by looking into the shadows and dispersing them with the light of knowledge, acceptance, and forgiveness. I learned that my story has not ended with Peter's death. I learned that this tenuous journey is part of the extraordinary labyrinth of life and that I want to travel its meandering, if at times perilous and painful, path. Most of all I have learned to respect and love the wondrous gift of Life.

> *Let us not burden our remembrance with*
> *A heaviness that's gone.*
>
> William Shakespeare

# Afterword

As my many diaries and scraps of paper lay around my house, they seemed to be an expression of my life. Bits and pieces were everywhere. Just as they have come together here to make some kind of order, so has my life.

Suicide leaves such a complicated mess, it is difficult to imagine the return of anything normal. It's one thing to know that you can move beyond suicide and another to know just how to do this. During the process of writing, I have had the opportunity to review my loss through a less immediate lens. I look back at how I felt and what I did, and I would like to share some of the more salient strategies that helped me.

- *Allow your family and friends to help you.* This will probably be absolutely necessary immediately. Not only can they help practically, they will be invaluable emotionally. Don't expect a smooth ride, though, as others will be experiencing their own emotional roller coaster. Be clear about your needs, as these must have priority, even when they change or appear unreasonable to others.

- *Seek specialized counseling.* Be aware that one size does not fit all. Try to find someone who is specifically experienced in suicide and with whom you relate. If you can't find the right person locally, don't be afraid to use the Internet. There is appropriate help available. You just need to find it.

- *Express your feelings.* Do this any way you can—through a diary, art, music, sports, talking with friends. It doesn't really matter how, but get those feelings out.

- *Do not make any major unalterable decisions immediately.* Give yourself time to accept the impact of what has happened.

- *Reframe some taken-for-granted perspectives.* For instance, disbelief is understandable, as suicide confronts our innate survival instinct and social values. While it may challenge core beliefs, deeper inspection might reveal suicide as part of the human condition and make it easier to accept.

- *Empower yourself through knowledge.* Find out as much as you are able about suicide to help understand your own situation.

- *Don't be hard on yourself.* Suicide was not your choice.

- *Recognize what your experience means.* Many senses can be violated by suicide. For instance, finding the body can leave powerful horrific imagery. Specialist help might be necessary to prevent this becoming embedded in your psyche.

- *Talk with your friends.* They want to help but may not know how to do this. Establish a safety link with someone, or several people, whom you can call frequently and at odd times.

- *Maintain your regular routines.* In the first instance, this may be difficult. You may need time off work if you are employed, and you may also need help to manage your daily life. Keeping your usual world functioning as well as you can provides some sense of continuity at a time when so much around you is changing.

- *Embrace your own way of grieving.* There is no set pattern or right or wrong way.

- *Do something for yourself regularly.* I found one of the most therapeutic things I did was having a regular massage. I was lucky enough to find an intuitive therapist. I got into the habit of having a massage late in the afternoon, close to home, so I didn't have to drive far and then coming home to a hot bath with the phone turned off. Thus I could gain full benefit from the relaxing massage and feel my grief in a deep way.

- *Walk, walk, and walk some more.* We are built to walk. Our bodies love it. So does our spirit. Wherever you are, whatever the demands of your daily life, incorporate walking into it. Simple things like parking a little way from your destination or choosing stairs instead of the escalator keep your body moving and functioning better.

- *Meditate every day.* This time-honored practice need not be fussy or time-consuming. You can incorporate simple techniques, such as mindfulness, to allow the peace within to calm you.

- *Try not to be overly introspective.* It is understandable to feel rejected or abandoned by the person who has suicided. Although it might feel personal, it is really about their pain, not you.

- *Remember the good times.* It can be difficult to recall the wonderful attributes of the person you loved if his or her entire life is reduced to those last moments. Rejoice in their life and what you shared with them.

- *Look after your health.* There may be times when you want to pig out on chocolate or have a few drinks too many, but make sure these times remain the exception rather than the rule. Eat and sleep well. Rest when you need to. Go swimming, try yoga—anything to keep your body functioning at its optimum.

- *Simplify your life.* At times of stress, it can be difficult to manage what once may have been easy. Don't get bogged down by things that don't mater any more. Prioritize essentials.

- *Don't lose contact with supportive friends.* Seek the company of those who boost you. Let less-supportive relationships slip away.

- *Learn to forgive.* This may not be easy, especially in the beginning. I found this step particularly difficult. It was only after I accepted that suicide is about pain relief that I was able free myself from the anxiety of my own culpability. Attaching blame is negative and destructive. Only love will help you move forward.

- *Choose acceptance, love, and forgiveness.* Empathize with the person you loved. Accept, love, and forgive that person. Accept, love, and forgive yourself. Accept, love, and forgive others.

- *Trust your inner spirit.* This is your greatest asset. Have faith that you have the strength within you to move beyond this life-altering experience in a positive way.

- *Do not let suicide define you.* You are not a victim, nor a survivor. You may have had a significant and terrible life experience, but it is only part of who you are.

- *Don't live in the past.* You can't change what has happened. You can only change what it means to you.

- *Embrace life.* Beyond suicide is *your* life. Love it and live it. Give yourself permission to be happy.

Wishing you peace as you walk in the wake of the suicide tsunami.

# About the Author

Sheralyn's lifelong interest in the social influences on health began in the jungles of Papua New Guinea in the early 1970s. Accompanying her husband there and subsequently to many parts of the world enabled her to work as a health practitioner and to use her PhD in medical sociology. She interpreted individual experiences of health as a reflection of a larger cultural picture and was able to incorporate this perspective into her work in health policy. Little did she imagine how closely her personal life would parallel her professional life. It is this juxtaposition that gave her the motivation to bring her intimate pain into a public space through *Suicide Tsunami*. She has now retired from the world of public health to garden and write in the mystical rainforest of Northern New South Wales. She lives there with her daughter, grandsons, pets, and the many wonderful creatures that call Australia home. She continues her association with people affected by suicide through personal consultation and through cyberspace.

www.suicidetsunami.com

# Suicide Help Lines

Australia

| | |
|---|---|
| Lifeline | 131-114 |
| Veterans and Veterans Families Counseling Service | 1800-011-046 |
| Mensline | 1300-789-978 |
| Kids Helpline | 1800-551-800 |
| Suicide Call Back Service | 1300-659-467 |
| Police/Ambulance | 000 (Mobile 112) |

Canada

| | |
|---|---|
| Suicide Hotline | 911 |
| | 1-800-784-2433 |
| | 1-800-448-1833 |

www.suicide.org
www.suicideprevention.ca

## Ireland

Samaritans

Life Line Northern Ireland
www.lifelinehelpline.info

1850-60-90-90
1850-60-90-91
0808-808-8000

## New Zealand

Lifeline Aotearoa Helpline
www.lifeline.org.nz
Suicide Prevention

0800-543-354

0508-828-865
0508-TANTOKO

## United Kingdom

Samaritans

www.samaritans.org
www.suicide.org
Military Veterans
Childline
SupportLine
HopeLine UK
www.papyrus.org.uk

+44 (0) 8457-90-90-90
+44 (0) 8457-90-91-92

1-800-273-TALK (press 1)
0800-1111
01708-765-200
0800-068-4141

## United States of America

National Suicide Prevention Lifeline    1-88-273-TALK (8255)
www.suicidepreventionlifeline.org
Hotline    1-800-784-2433
www.suicidehotlines.com

# CONTRIBUTORS

Carole, whose lover of nine years gassed himself in his car
Carrie, whose husband suicided after years of depression and PTSD
Evan, whose partner drowned herself in the bath
Gina, whose partner of fifteen years shot himself
James, whose sister threw herself from the roof of her apartment after leaving a suicide note; she died in a hospital five days after her fall
Joanne, whose cousin completed suicide after three attempts
Ken, Section Commander with Peter in South Vietnam
Lin, whose adult son suicided
Lisa, whose twenty-year-old brother jumped to his death from a cliff
Mia, whose husband of thirty-six years hanged himself at home while she slept
Nellie, whose boyfriend shot himself in their flat; she currently is in a counseling program
Petra, whose daughter is missing, presumed dead from suicide
Rob, whose father, Peter, suicided
Rowena, whose husband shot himself, leaving her with two small children
Sharon, whose husband of thirty-four years hanged himself after struggling with depression for many years
Tammy, whose partner gassed himself in his car

Tiffany, whose sister suicided when she was twenty-seven; since being interviewed, Tiffany has sought help, is now back at work, and is no longer suicidal

Tim and Mary, whose twenty-four-year-old son shot himself

Tracey, whose boyfriend, Joe, threw himself from a headland

# References

Albom, Mitch, (2005), *Tuesdays with Morrie*, Hodder Headline Australia, Sydney.

Albom, Mitch, (2009), *Have a Little Faith*, Sphere, London.

American Foundation for Suicide Prevention, (2003), "Survivor Research: AFSP and NIMH Propose Research Agenda for Survivors of Suicide."

Barnes, Julian, (2011), *The Sense of an Ending*, Jonathan Cape, London.

Cantwell-Bartl, Annie, (2003), "Is this Person Suffering from Grief or Trauma or Traumatic Grief?" www.cismfa.org.au

Barford, Philip, *Urlicht,* in Mahler, G., 2 Resurrection.

Clark, David, (2005), Center for Suicide Research and Prevention, Religion and Ethics Newsweekly, Episode 908.

Clark, Sheila, (1995), *After Suicide: Help for the Bereaved*, Hill of Content, Melbourne.

Cutler, H. C. and the Dalai Lama, (1998), *The Art of Happiness. A Handbook for Living*, Riverhead Hardcover.

Davidson, Richard J, with Begley, Sharon, (2013), *The Emotional Life of Your Brain,* Hodder and Stoughton Ltd., London.

Didion, Joan, (2005), *The Year of Magical Thinking*, Fourth Estate, London.

Donne, John, (1624), Devotions upon Emergent Occasions, No 17.

Doidge, Norman, (2007), *The Brain that Changes Itself,* Scribe, Melbourne.

Fine, Carla, (1997), *No Time to say Good-bye: Surviving the Suicide of a Loved One*, Broadway Books, New York.

Geddes and Grosset, (1996), *English Dictionary*, David Dale House, Scotland.

Goldman, Linda, (2001), *Breaking the Silence*, Routledge, New York and London.

Granello, D.H. and Granello, P.F., (2007), *Suicide: An Essential Guide for Helping Professionals and Educators*, Merrill, an imprint of Pearson Education Inc.

Gray Sexton, Linda, (2011: pp. 181–193), *Half in Love. Surviving the legacy of suicide*, Counterpoint, Berkeley, CA.

Grens, L., (2011), "Murder, Suicide Top Medical Deaths in Pregnancy," Thomson Reuters.

Griffiths, Trevor, (2010), "Emotional Chaos Theory," http://emotionalchaostheory.blogspot.com

Grashoff, Udo, (2007), *Let Me Finish*, Headline Publishing Group, London.

Hawton, K., and Heeringen, K., (18/4/2009), "Suicide," The Lancet, Vol. 373, Issue 9672, pp.1372–1381.

Honore, Christophe, (2006), "Inside Paris," Madman Film.

Jacobs, Selby, (1999), *Traumatic Grief: Diagnosis, Treatment and Prevention*, Hamilton Printing Co., Castleton, NY.

Kennedy, Alexandra, (2001), *The Infinite Thread: Healing Relationships Beyond Loss*, Beyond Words, Oregon.

Kinchin, David, (2004), *Post-Traumatic Stress Disorder. The Invisible Injury*, Success Unlimited, Great Britain.

Korngold, Jussara, (2006), *Those Left Behind: Understanding Suicide from a Spiritist View*, iUniverse, New York.

Krauss, Lawrence, (2009) "A Universe From Nothing," University of Arizona.

Leader, Darian, ((2008), *The New Black. Mourning, Melancholia and Depression*, Penguin, London.

Leslie-Adams, Adele, (1999), "I thought it was just me …," Vietnam Veterans Counseling Service, Australia.

Lukas, Christopher and Seiden, Henry M., (2007), *Silent Grief: Living in the Wake of Suicide*, Jessica Kingsley Publishers, London.

MacKellar, Maggie, (2010), *When it Rains*, Vintage Press, Australia.

McLean, Don, "Vincent."

Moran, Lord, (1945, 1966, 1987), *The Anatomy of Courage: The Classic Study of the Soldier's Struggle Against Fear*, Avery Publishing Grouping Inc., New York.

Morgan, Tom, (2009), "Why a Broken Heart Can Kill," Daily Express, London (p.29).

Morris Coryell, Deborah, (2007), *Good Grief: Healing Through the Shadow of Loss*, Healing Arts Press, Rochester, Vermont.

Mueller Bryson, Karen, (2006), *Those Left Behind: Interviews, Stories, Essays and Poems by Survivors of Suicide*, Lulu, USA.

Myers, Michael F., and Fine, Carla, (2006), *Touched by Suicide: Hope and Healing After Loss*, Gotham Books, New York.

Nyman, Michael, *If*, song from *The Diary of Anne Frank*, Roger Pulvers.

O'Donohue, John, *Anam Cara*, (1997), Harper Perennial, New York.

Owen, Wilfred, (1917), *Anthem for Doomed Youth*.

Pope, Alexander, (1733-4), *An Essay on Man*. Epistle 1.

Robinson, Ken, (2010), *The Element. How Finding Your Passion Changes Everything*, Penguin Books Limited, London.

Robinson, Rita, (2001), *Survivors of Suicide*, New Page Books, Franklin Lakes, NJ.

Rollin, B., (2005), "Religion and Ethics Newsweekly," Episode 908.

Ryan, Roma, "If I Could Be Where You Are," Enya.

Ross, Eleanora Betsy, (1997), *After Suicide: A ray of hope for those left behind*, Da Capo Press, Cambridge, MA.

Safe TALK: Suicide alertness for everyone.

Salratore, Tony, (2008), "Suicide Loss FAQs," www.lifegard.tripod.com

Shakespeare, William, (1605), *Hamlet*, Act I, scene iii.

Shakespeare, William, (1605), *Macbeth,* Act IV, scene iii.
Shakespeare, William, (1605), *Tempset,* Act 1, scene i.
Shneidman, Edwin S., (2004), *Autopsy of a Suicidal Mind,* Oxford University Press, New York.
Smutz, J.C., (1926, 1961, 1999), *Holism and Evolution,* MacMillan.
Sparrow, Ginny, (2003), American Association of Suicidology.
Sternberg, Ester M., (2009), *Healing Spaces: The Science of Place and Well-Being,* Harvard University Press.
Stroebe, Margaret; Stroebe, Wolfgang; and Hansson, Robert, (1999), *Handbook of Bereavement: Theory, Research, and Intervention,* Cambridge University Press, USA.
Tatz, C., (1999), "Aboriginal Suicide is Different," Criminal Research Council Grant; (25/96-7).
Tolle, Eckhart, (1999), *The Power of Now. A Guide to Spiritual Enlightenment,* Namaste Publishing, California.
Weber, Zita Annette, (2000), *Out of the Blues,* Margaret Gee, Australia.
Williams, Robbie, *Better Man,* Robbie Williams Lyrics.
Wolpert, Lewis, (2001), *Malignant Sadness: The Anatomy of Depression,* Faber and Faber, London.
Wood, Tony and Siler, Steve, (2003), *Chaos of the Heart: Grieving a Suicide,* New Spring-Publishing ASCAP/Silerland Music ASCAP.
www.choselife.net
www.livingworks.net
www.monash.edu.au
www.nosp.ie
www.omh.ny.gov
www.suicidefirstaid.org.au

Made in the USA
Lexington, KY
06 July 2016